About the Author

Rex Wood is a 30-year-old regular guy from Ealing in West London. He has a day job in Investment Banking. He has been a regular on the London dating scene for several years. He has also been in and out of several serious and non-serious relationships. He also contributes to several dating blogs where users seek advice on how to handle challenges in their relationships. In his spare time, Rex plays Football and Tennis. He was also a member of a Drama Club when he was younger.

For more information or to get in touch with Rex, Please email rexwoodauthor@gmail.com

REX WOOD

Sexcellence
The Sex Spreadsheet

To my lovely Bella and to all my wingmen and wingwomen

AUTHOR'S NOTE

This book is a work of memoir. It is a true story based on my best recollections of various events in my life. The names and identifying characteristics of certain people have been changed in order to protect their privacy. In some instances, I rearranged and/or compressed events and time periods in service of the narrative, and I recreated dialogue to match my best recollection of those exchanges.

Copyright © Rex Wood 2017

The right of Rex Wood to be identified as the Author of the Work has been asserted by him in accordance with the Copyright, Designs and Patents Act 1988.

All rights reserved. No part of this publication may be reproduced, stored in a retrieval system, or transmitted, in any form or by any means without the prior written permission of the publisher, nor be otherwise circulated in any form of binding or cover other than that in which it is published and without a similar condition being imposed on the subsequent purchases.

ROW 1

INTRODUCTION

THE SPREADSHEET

Wow! So where do I start? This is my first ever book. There was never a plan to do this, but I thought it would be great to share my personal experiences.

This is not really meant to be a guide to picking up girls or guys or anything like that, but it could possibly serve as one. But I feel like different techniques work for different people so I will not really be focusing only on that aspect of things. However, there might be tips you might pick up which might be helpful as you look to maximize your potential with the opposite sex.

Take a second to think of this. All men could sleep with thousands of girls if they actually wanted to. There are millions of women in London alone. I can gladly say that I have slept with possibly 90% of the women I went on a date with and 99% of those who made it to the second date. So essentially, I am saying that it is not actually that bad if you do not pick up a girl on the first night in a club for example.

As you read through the book you can take some notes and make decisions as to what works for you as you look to become a man like me who has had sex with over a hundred girls. This is not a very large number by any means, but I feel like I could share my experiences and add value to those who maybe feel like they could do better in this "game."

Let me talk a bit about my spreadsheet. The actual spreadsheet idea came up a few years ago when I decided to be honest with myself and actually figure out how many women I had slept with. I started with a sheet of A4 paper. Front and back, I filled it up with maybe 60 names and then I eventually moved the list on to an Excel spreadsheet where I could update it and track it more efficiently.

I also liked to perform statistical analysis. For example, the most common name for my sexual conquests was "Emma". So, whenever I met a girl called Emma ever since I did this analysis, I thought to myself "Hi Emma, well... I am statistically more likely to smash you tonight than anyone else and I have the numbers to prove it... ha ha."

Another statistic which was very obvious was that my wildest and most incredible smashes were with Americans. I listed out a few quotes. This goes back to the first American girl I ever smashed back at university in 2005. We were watching a movie and hanging out for the first time. She paused, closed the laptop and was like "Rex are you gonna fuck me or what?" Ha ha - I froze and was instantly extremely turned on.

In this book, I share details of 69 rows of my spreadsheet in a chronological order. I start off very "kiss and tell" and as you read further down the rows, I talk more about strategy, and more specifically pulling and dating techniques.

ROW 2

CANDY SHOP

AUGUST 2005

I met Lucy on the streets of Belfast while I was working as a charity fundraiser. I had stopped her more attractive sister with the intention of signing her up to the charity. I do not remember being particularly attracted to her at the time.

Sometimes as a young man I tended to respond to female attention with the question 'Would I smash her or not?' As a horny 19-year-old, the answer was 'Yes' most of the time. I am not going to exactly say that I was fucking the hottest girls around at those times. I mean I did get my fair share of decent pussy, but let's just say my standard deviation of quality of girls was quite large.

I signed Lucy's sister up to the charity and she ended up mentioning that her sister fancied me. As she had already passed the 'Smash Test,' it was a case of execution. At this point, I was a wild teenager who was away from home for the first time. I was not particularly experienced in the dating or sex game. What I had though was supreme confidence which I definitely contributed to my consistent success with girls in my sex career.

Armed with the knowledge that Lucy fancied me, I spoke to her with confidence and told her I was in town for a few days and that I really liked the city of Belfast. We had a chat for about 15 minutes, and as the Northern Ireland rain poured down, we exchanged numbers at the entrance of a store in the city centre. Considering I had also signed her sister up, this was proving to be an all-around win.

Later that evening, I had been texting Lucy, and she had arranged to come over to the house I was staying on Malone Avenue. It was a large five bedroom house in a pretty decent area of Belfast. I had one of the large ensuite rooms downstairs and I had turned this into a sort of temporary bachelor pad. The bedroom had this old school audio deck style set up which was hooked up to a CD player. The kitchen was just next door and there was an adjoining door which led to an amazing garden. This was all nicely set up for a romantic date. A romantic smash if you would like.

To be honest, as guys we do like to use these aggressive words about sex to make us appear more manly and masculine with each other. Words like bang, destroy, annihilate, smash and many more, when in actual fact, I have only ever touched, licked and treated every single pussy with excellent care, attention and pleasure.

Lucy arrived at the house at about 8pm. The young lady came armed with a bottle of Smirnoff Vodka. These were obviously the days before Grey Goose, Ciroc, Belvedere and Effen. It was a decent start to the evening; I had ordered a Chinese takeaway and was sipping on a can of beer. Funnily enough, I had also picked up 50 Cent's "The Massacre" album. This was a 22-track album which was doing very well at the time. There was one particular song which Lucy really liked. It was called 'Candy Shop'. I could not have written this script any better, but it is still all very fresh in my memory even though it was about 12 years ago.

So, I put the album on, starting with the first track while we ate and drank. After a couple of tracks, I had Lucy on my lap and we started kissing passionately. It may seem very obvious but I do not really remember ever having sex with a girl without starting off with a kiss. Exceptions to this could be if she had really bad teeth or something. This actually happened to me once as you will find out later on in this book.

So, with Lucy on my lap and 50 Cent's album playing and vodka flowing, you could imagine how cosy and perfectly set up this was for a wild evening.

Lucy was on top of me dancing and pretty much giving me a lap dance. It felt great and naturally led to a massive hard-on. This was then the 'point of no return' as once she felt my erection she was turned on herself and she started to use her hands and rub my penis aggressively.

She was the one doing the destruction here, so she did that for a few minutes and then she pulled my tracksuit bottoms down. Yes tracksuit bottoms - at that young age of 19, I always used to set things up a bit so that a girl felt my erection first and so it got her thinking or in the right mood. Wearing tracksuit bottoms when having girls around always did that because track pants were less fitting on the body.

She took my bottoms off and slid my hard cock into her mouth. She then stroked it with her hands and sucked it extremely pleasantly. We ended up having sex on the floor.

Lucy was a smoker and so after the first round of sex we went out into the garden as she had a cigarette and we watched the stars and spoke. The first conversations I have after sex with a new girl are always very genuine. The reason for this is that I usually overcome my initial instincts and sexual desires. We had a good conversation about her life and her job and the challenges she was facing in life.

We then went back into the room and the idea of making a sex video seemed extremely appealing. I set up a chair behind the door and positioned my black Nokia 6230 on the audio deck. I turned the music on to track seven, 'Candy Shop', and I sat on the chair.

In good view of the camera and while singing and shaking her curvy body to the track, Lucy sat on top of me and we had sex on tape. To help you picture this, you could perhaps listen to the track and imagine Lucy riding me while the lyrics 'I'll take you to the candy shop, I'll let you lick the lollipop...' are playing.

This was a very fun night, and the first of several nights spent with over a hundred girls in my life so far. After all the sex and vodka, we were both pretty tired and we actually both fell asleep on the floor, leaving the bed empty.

The next morning I woke up and made my guest a nice breakfast of a toast with peanut butter and coffee. She then left as I believe she had to get to work. I was left with memories of a great night, both in my mind and on my phone. I had made my first ever sex tape. This was to be shared amongst several friends and colleagues at the University. Looking back, I do regret that. However, it was great entertainment and part of the excitement of this new experience I was having.

ROW 3

INTRODUCTION TO NORTH-AMERICA

OCTOBER 2005

Before I get to Anita, the next name on the spreadsheet, I would like to explain how I was evolving as a man in other areas of my life as well. As the saying goes, "He is much more than just a pretty face". When I enrolled at University after "The Summer of Lucy", I was clearly eager to make an impression with my new mates. It was a Sunday evening at the end of September; I had been dropped off at the Halls of Residence in Central London by my family.

I started off the evening dropping off my bags before meeting my flatmates and then heading over to the student bar around the corner. At the bar, there was a freshers' welcome night and I wasted no time in making friends. The worst part of this was that, for every three guy friends I made, I had probably shared the Lucy video with one of them.

I am not sure whether I understood or completely grew up with the desire to have an image as a playboy. I certainly was heading that way with the reputation created from the video. Word spread quickly, my room became called 'The Candy Shop', and I became known as the guy who loved women and liked sex a lot. As if that does not apply to all men. I must say, from that experience I was seen as even more desirable to several girls. I am not a proverbial man, but they do also say that "women love bad boys" and "treat them mean to keep them keen".

The reputation I was building up certainly helped me earn the respect of every single guy who knew me or had met me at the University. I was even invited to join the University's social committee to help organize parties and nights out. All this from a three-minute sex video. I am not saying I lasted only three minutes. Well, maybe I did, but Lucy did put the work in and so she was certainly partly responsible for that.

I lived with a bunch of girls and a couple of guys. We had a good flat and all got on really well. The girls even at one point played a prank on me and decorated my room with candy, as well as labelling my door with the words 'The Candy Shop' using a few bags of Tesco Pick 'n Mix. While still enjoying the first few weeks of the term including all the midweek booze-fests and nights out, my notoriety grew from 'one sex tape'.

On one midweek evening, I and a bunch of my flatmates had gone out to a club called 'Moonlighting' on Greek Street in Soho. My flatmate Anwyn had brought a friend from her course along. If I thought I was wild and crazy, if you reading this book think you are wild and crazy, we would both be nothing compared to her friend Anita. Anita was a wild Canadian redhead

- the first interesting entry into the 'Hair Colour' column of the spreadsheet.

We had a wild night of dancing and drinking at the club. This was fairly reasonable as drinks on those student nights cost 50 pence. At the time, this was equivalent to around 90 American Cents. We all know what happens - cheap drinks lead to students getting wasted, kissing each other, and a fair amount of sex does occur after most of these nights.

To put this set up into perspective, there was a fellow student of mine at the time, a young lady called Zainab, who always wore her full Muslim gear. I believe she had decided to try alcohol for the first time in her life. By the end of the night, she was pole-dancing wildly in the club with her Hijab still on. This did cause a lot of joy and laughter, but it was all fun and games. This was how happy and friendly the atmosphere was.

Perhaps Zainab was the only one wilder than Anita on that night. Anita was grinding all night, both with the air and with any guy who came within one square metre of her. I was waiting like a hyena ready to pounce. I kind of kept my distance without actually keeping my distance. The way you do this is to be around her in the same group of people, whilst not paying her any attention at all. So you pay attention to everyone else and make her work hard for your attention. I showed a perfect execution of this principle with Anita.

With about ten minutes to go until the club closed, she backed me up with her ass and pushed me against the wall. Whilst with my back to the wall, she derided aggressively against my crotch. This led to an instant erection and even felt like my dick was about to fall off.

We left the club and got the night bus back to our Halls of Residence. I was feeling confident as I had kissed Anita just before we left the club. So for me, once there has been a kiss, then the door is wide open.

We got back to the halls and she came straight to my room. It was funny: I was buzzing and everything was perfect. We got into my room and she asked for a towel. I was like 'err... well okay' and I handed her one. I was literally thinking, 'Does this young lady actually just want to come here, have a shower and go?' Well, the actual words in my head were more like, 'Does this bitch... bla bla bla'.

She came back to my room 15 minutes later, wrapped in my purple towel, her red hair all dripping wet and giving me that look. She took the towel off and lay naked on my bed on her back and was like 'Rex I just want you to fuck me' in her amazing Canadian accent. Oh my God I love girls so much; you are the greatest creations of all, or the greatest results of all evolution, whatever your belief is.

Anita had an amazing ass, incredible tits, and great thighs. I could not believe my luck. I took my clothes off instantly and went on top of her and fucked her to the best of my ability. She was so loud, so loud that my next door neighbour kept banging on the wall. We had sex for about half an hour and then we took a break.

The way the room was laid out, it was like your typical ensuite dorm room. It had a desk parallel to the bed. The desk had a chair which was meant for work. Well, work could mean anything. The only work that was done on that chair that evening was me inserting my dick in and out my Canadian friend's pussy.

There were shades of my previous experience with Lucy here. Sex with Rex on a chair while making a sex tape. As you can guess, due to the huge success of the first video I made, I whipped my phone out and asked Anita if she would mind having sex on tape. By the way guys and girls, you should never record sex without your partner's consent. I am not an advocate of any of that as it usually ends badly.

Anita and I made a trade; she agreed that I could film us having sex if she could get a naked picture of me. She liked my bum, so she wanted a side profile showing my bum and my hard dick. I gladly obliged and allowed her to take the picture. Back in those days, there was no Snapchat, so there was no risk of her creating a live snap of our sex without me knowing. I hope I am giving you bad ideas and triggering your inner dirty minds.

I whipped my phone out, sat on the chair and Anita rode and rode me. I recorded it with the phone in my hand. We literally just messed about on camera. She stood up, sat on me backwards and we did reverse cowgirl. She then turned back around and rode me again and she said 'Hi Mum' on camera. I just hope the video never got to her mum through its journey through cyberspace.

We fucked on camera until I came and sprayed all over her huge 32DD tits. Believe me, this video was a major hit. I had my phone taken from my room several times by several college mates wanting to see the video after I had shown it to a couple of friends.

Anita actually mentioned to me that she did not mind me showing the video around. If you ask me, I think this girl wanted to be a porn star deep inside. I was more than glad to be her acting partner. I never spoke to her or saw her again after that night. She more than deserved a place on my spreadsheet for giving me and showing me an intense night of passion and great sex, and also my first experience with a redhead. I would like to give a massive shout-out to all the redheads reading this book.

ROW 4

AMERICAN OBSESSION

MARCH 2006

There I was, the party boy on campus. Two successful sex videos, some of which were even uploaded by an unknown person on to the exclusive campus platform called DC++.

What made my videos different was the excitement of the girls to be in them. It was like a celebration of equality, where on both occasions, both girls enjoyed being filmed. They had such pride and confidence in their bodies that they were willing to share them with the world and I highly respected that.

School, classes, bars, clubs, kitchen parties and more bars. This was the kind of lifestyle I was living. One evening in March, I was invited to a party in a room of a guy who I had met on campus. His name was Phillip. He was a cool Croatian kid, tall and very handsome with blonde hair. You see us guys we stick together.

The best way to attract the largest amount of attractive girls is by having a bunch of attractive guys in a room. I do appreciate when I see a guy who is good looking most of the time and I definitely would gladly compliment him. I have no issues or qualms with that. On this Saturday evening, it was all set to be a good one. Girls, booze, music, cosy room. What a fucking amazing set up for a wild party. Haha... I know what you are thinking, but no it did not end up being one of those "eyes wide shut" frat parties.

Well, a bunch of us walked down the road to a 24-hour supermarket to buy alcohol. There was enough booze for about a hundred people to get absolutely wasted even though the room party had maybe about 20 people. So, essentially, each party attendee in Phillip's room could get wasted five times over. These were the levels we were drinking at.

We drank and drank all night; I met a few girls in the room party who I got on well with. There was Zoe, a hot brunette who spent the whole evening dancing on my lap. Who needed the strip club, when you could be a cool 19-year-old having all these chicks grinding on you every single day? This was "the life."

At Phillip's room party, there was also a girl called Claire. She was an Italian-American on a year abroad. Dark hair, amazing blue eyes, lips that would force any man or woman to fantasize about what they could be potentially used for. When Zoe got off my lap, I approached Claire and spoke to her. I think I even described her as a hot "Amy Lee." Amy is the lead singer of an American group called "Evanescence." The compliment brought her to life. See what I did there?

Well, Claire and I were getting on really well; I am not sure how the rest of the party went as I was too wasted to remember. However, what I do know was that I had laid a seed for what could be another great sexual experience. Sexual Rex was taking things to the next level. I had seen Claire out and about after the party and I always made eye contact and said hi. I played it cool. You have to play it cool most of the time and then wait for your opportunity to pounce.

There was one day I was walking into my dorm. There was a payphone on the left as you walked in. On this day, it was Claire who was sitting there on the phone. She was wearing pink pyjamas of which the bottom half were like hot pants. "Oh my God!" I went a bit crazy after seeing those amazing legs and thighs.

It was time to make something happen. Enough of saying hi and enough small talk in the hallway. How was I going to do this? I promised myself I would ask for her number the next time I saw her. Maybe this is what might have delayed my smash with her - I had not asked for her number at the party when we met. It was my way of playing cool as I was confident we would cross paths as we lived in the same dorm.

Seeing her on the pay phone, I went into the adjoining TV room which had glass doors. I turned on the TV and started watching a show. It's not like I was that interested in the show. I used that to pass time while I waited to pounce. The moment she got off the phone I got up and went over to her and asked how she was and how she was enjoying London. I told her I hoped she wasn't missing her family too much. We swapped numbers, both room telephone, and mobile numbers. I was about to "lock this down."

I texted Claire on a Friday and she invited me to go to her room the following Sunday evening to watch a movie. When Sunday arrived, a few of the guys in the dorm and I decided to go over to a park just around the corner to play football. We played for about an hour and a half. I played with a smile knowing what I had planned for that evening. It was also a nice little cardiovascular warm up for what was about to happen that night.

After the game, I went back to my room and had a shower. There were two missed calls on my phone, and guess what, the girl was getting impatient. She was asking if I could come earlier and where I was. I kept my composure and texted her saying I was running late as I had been playing football.

For guys reading this, it always helps to appear busy and have a life when dealing with girls. It is pretty basic advice, but trust me it is key. I took my time, got ready, and put my Nike track pants on. These were the same pair I wore with Lucy in Belfast and it will not be the last time you hear of them in this book.

I took the lift up to the fifth floor where Claire's room was. She was 21 at the time and was on the floor with the rest of the postgrads. I thought "What a cougar."

I remembered one Friday evening when my friend Craig and I went up to the roof of the dorm while we were high on something. We actually did see some fifth-floor action through someone's partially open curtains. The fifth floor was definitely home to the more experienced and I was about to test myself.

I walked into Claire's room. It smelled very nicely of her Davidoff "Cool Water" fragrance. That smell turns me on (well it did back in the day anyway). I unpacked my laptop bag and placed the laptop on her desk.

We sat on her bed side to side with our backs against the wall all set to watch a movie. I put "The Matrix" on - the first of the trilogy. It was a good way to start as I actually did like the movie. Always choose a movie you like otherwise you will get restless if you are trying to bed a girl and you watch a movie you don't like.

We were maybe an hour into the movie, Neo and Morpheus were keeping me entertained, I was laughing and joking with Claire, and I am not too sure what happened but I had a massive erection and her hand struck it randomly at some point. I was like "oops" and I saw the shock on her face. It was shock filled with excitement and curiosity. I waited five minutes and I went in for the kiss.

Again, it always starts with a kiss. Once we made out for a bit, I paused to try and play it cool and watched a bit more of the movie. She grabbed me and said "Rex are you going to fuck me or what?"

Quickly, the grey track pants came down and she sucked my dick in the best way I could ever imagine: on her knees on a pillow, both hands on my butt, lips round my cock. In and out, in and out. It was the best foreplay I had ever had. She stood up and I licked her out. It was my first time licking a girl out, but I had watched so much porn by this point that the only thing I didn't know was the taste. Her pussy tasted really good and I could have licked her out all night.

She wanted me to fuck the shit out of her. I wanted to oblige, but at this point, I realized I had no condoms on me. Oh my goodness, what a spoiler. I dashed out of her room downstairs straight to the lift and ran to my flatmate's room, still hard and with visible pre-cum. My flatmate Eamon was very reliable. I have no idea why he even had condoms; he never had sex. I heard he is married with a kid now but I am pretty sure he lost his virginity on his wedding night.

Anyway, I grabbed about three Durex condoms. I dashed down the corridor; imagine if there was a fire alarm or anything that would have denied me of this! I would have gone absolutely crazy. I thought to myself. "From now on Rex, you will carry two condoms in your wallet at all times."

I made it back to her room in time. She was still so horny, as was I. We didn't even need to repeat foreplay, she just lay down and I went straight in and fucked her. We fucked on the bed, on the chair, doggy style against the sink and she also rode me on the floor. At some point, she ripped the condom off and I fucked her bareback. Very naughty.

She said to me, "Don't put it in my ass like Phillip did." Oh my God, so she actually fucked Phillip the night I met her. I just thought "Well at least I'm fucking you now" and it even spurred me on to fuck her better. I came so many times: once in her mouth, once on her tits and the old school withdrawal and that went all over her chest and stomach. Claire is one of my favourite ladies on the spreadsheet.

She confessed that she had heard about my videos and that made her want to fuck me even more. She also said she wouldn't mind me filming, but at this point, I had had enough of that reputation. I preferred all memories of our sex experiences to be left in our minds, and maybe on an Excel spreadsheet later on in our lives.

ROW 5

THE VICTIMISATION OF REX

MARCH 2006

It was the Easter holidays. Most of us had gone home with the intention of coming back after three weeks. Halfway through the three weeks, I spoke to a couple of my friends and we were already bored of home and missing University. We then arranged for drinks on Friday which was a couple of days later.

The drinks were actually planned for the daytime and so we started off at about 4pm. It was casual pints of beer, which then became cheeky snakebites and then spirits as the sun set, shots back to snakebites and then jaeger-bombs and absynth. I was absolutely fucking smashed.

In our group, there were three guys and three girls drinking that day. One of the girls was Anna. I had just met her that afternoon. To be honest I wouldn't even say I had met her. She was drinking with us as she knew my friend Ivan as they shared the same dorm. I probably only said "hi" to her in the introduction. In the nicest possible way to put it, she wasn't exactly "my cup of tea" from a physical point of view. Rex was about to venture into a night he will regret for the rest of his life. The best out of that night would perhaps be the giggle that readers would get from reading this row.

It was a night which my friends who knew of it have never dropped despite it occurring 11 years ago. So, back to the story, it was maybe about 1am. We had been drinking for nine hours. I was absolutely smashed. I went back to Ivan's room after the bar. I left his room and stumbled across the hall out of the flat and to the elevator. My plan was to head back to my place.

As I got there, I pushed the elevator button maybe getting it right on the third attempt. The elevator bleeped, the doors open and a huge figure appeared in front of me. From my drunken memory, she was huge both in height and in width. Not that there is anything wrong with a woman of that size. In my state, she appeared so much larger than I had imagined. I remember her being so happy to see me.

She asked "Rex, where are you going?". I responded whilst stumbling in my mumbling drunk voice. "I going home". Ha ha... I don't remember if I said it like that, as I was too drunk to an extent I couldn't even hear myself. I just know I uttered some words which meant "a la casa" or "a chez-moi" in my head. That means home by the way. Anna responded "No you are too drunk to go home by yourself". She laid down the hammer.

Fuck me I was in for fun that night. Think of the list of alcoholic drinks I mentioned earlier and mixing all that up. I was bound to puke at some point. Right? The moment to puke came. It was like the perfect timing, like surely she was not going to hit on me if I puked.

She pushed me against the wall and started kissing me. I was too weak to reject the kiss so I kissed along. About five seconds in, I said to her "I gonna be sick". I then broke loose from her and ran off back into the flat to throw up. I found the kitchen sink and threw up a cocktail of puke into it. I felt better, it was such a relief getting all that out.

So you wouldn't believe what happened next. Anna came over and started clearing the sink of my sick with her bare hands. In my drunk state, I was like "No way, there's no way she is doing that" she cleared the whole thing out. I was so impressed at her hospitality towards me. But like she could have at least used a tissue or a pair of kitchen gloves or anything else for that matter. It kind of spelt out the mood she was in at that point. She was down to get her hands dirty in more ways than one.

After she had cleaned my sick, she then took me to her room. We got into her room and she handed me her toothbrush. It was her personal toothbrush and not a spare. She said "Why don't you brush your teeth and come into bed?" I used her toothbrush and cleaned my mouth to get rid of all the sick.

I then got into her bed and she came on top of me and started kissing me. Remember this was a girl I wasn't attracted to in any way, but I obliged to the kissing. This only happened due to the extremely drunk state I found myself in. I feel like she knew this, but then she asked me if I wanted to have sex. I said "Yes". She then started to give me oral sex to try and get me up. I got hard by thinking constantly of "Jennifer Lopez" yes "J.Lo". This worked and Anna was able to go on top of me and ride me.

I woke up the next day not knowing where I was for a moment. I just remember seeing this huge figure next to me and I was laying in her shadow. For me, this was just a lesson. I had let my drunkenness get in the way of my judgement. Because of this, I ended up having sex with a girl I had no attraction to. Well, it was definitely a funny experience and I thank Anna for taking care of me and cleaning my sick. She made it onto the spreadsheet against all odds so I give her credit for that. The last thing I heard about her was that she became a lesbian a few months later.

ROW 6

CAN A GUY AND A GIRL REALLY BE FRIENDS?

MAY 2006

I was back at university for the last term of my first year. I always had a flirtatious relationship with some of the girls in my dorms as expected. I blame it mainly on my videos and my mannerism and swagger. If you go back to "Anita', the third girl on my spreadsheet, you would see that she was introduced to me by Anwyn, my welsh flatmate.
Due to the fact that we were flatmates, I never really considered her as a sexual partner. Our relationship was more like friends than anything. Although we did have the odd grind whilst we were out clubbing. She did have an amazing ass and she always wore short skirts around the flat and in the kitchen. Sometimes she would just come to my room in a short skirt and sit on my bed and chat. She would even come and lay next to me while I was having a nap just to have a friendly chat.

This potentially opens up a whole new debate about whether guys and girls can truly be friends. Obviously on the surface as long as you both know that you are just friends and there are no extremely testing situations then it is okay. The moment that is ever breached, Can you still say you are friends? I think not.

A lot of girls tell me that this guy or that guy is their friend. Do you know what I say to them? I say "try and give him a blow job and if he says no firmly and does not oblige then he is truly a friend". How many girls would like to risk trying that though? Probably none. So, we would probably never truly find out the answer to this question in most cases.

Anwyn had pushed me to the limit. I was still quite young and inexperienced then, but if it was like today I can say I would probably have fucked her within the first 15 minutes of meeting her. To start with, she spent so much time in my room, and not in a friendly way, like she would knock on my door and see in my boxers and on my desk working on my laptop and she would come and sit on my lap to chat. It was actually quite ridiculous.

To be honest it didn't help that her room was actually next door to mine and she would have heard me have sex with other girls, including her friend Anita who she literally fed on a plate to me.

I could safely and confidently conclude that she wanted a piece of me. It couldn't have been more obvious. But obviously, I never wanted to ruin the friendship we had because at the same time it is always very nice to have female friends. But not like this, not one who was almost always going out of her way to turn you on at every opportunity.

This all had to come to an end. And I tell you it did, otherwise she would not have been on the spreadsheet obviously. We went out drinking one evening. I remember we started dancing together.

Think of all the months of sexual tension building up. We were now drunk on a dancefloor somewhere in London. We were both obviously turned on. We were both also perhaps scared to be the first to make that step which would most definitely end our status as friends. I think it was scarier thinking what our other friends and flatmates would say. Well, I didn't care that much. My mindset was getting my dick wet as with most guys whether they would like to admit it or not.

So we were dancing and then our lips touched and we locked lips and tongues and everything. We both had hands all over each other, and it was going great. The next thing I knew, one of our mutual friends Becky grabbed Anwyn away from me on the dancefloor. That was the end of our fun that night.

Becky did it to prevent us from doing something we would both 'regret'. I understood where she was coming from, but really we were all kids here and I didn't appreciate being "cock-blocked" like that. But I was fine with it as I knew I would end up bedding her in no time. Especially if she continued her seduction process with me as she was doing.

The next morning I was in the kitchen making breakfast and wearing a tee-shirt and some Umbro sports shorts with no boxers underneath. I was making an omelette, and guess who walked in, it was Anwyn. She proceeded to hug me and we flirted a bit. Actually a lot. I had my breakfast and then I left her and went into my room.

I was in my room for maybe ten minutes when I heard a knock on the door. Yes, you know who it was. She walked in and I locked the door. She laid on my bed while I sat up and had my hands straight under her skirt. She then proceeded to give me a blowjob while saying "we shouldn't be doing this". Ha ha... that part was hilarious.

I ended up fucking her and it was definitely worth the wait. We had great sex that afternoon and night as well. But then I think I was then put off by her "promiscuity" as I later found out she had slept with about three other guys in the same dorm.

We went back to being friends, and I think we were better friends afterwards than we were before as we had sex to remove all forms of sexual tension and build up.

Obviously, that happened by chance and would definitely not work in all cases. But it definitely worked for her and she became the first Welsh name on my spreadsheet. I was nearly completing the union-jack of pussy with my Irish, Welsh, and English names on there.

ROW 7

TRAVEL ANYWHERE FOR "IT"

JULY 2006

Here we are, until now I had shagged a few girls in my first year at the university and I had a fuck buddy called Claire from one of the previous rows on the spreadsheet. I was fucking Claire maybe for the rest of my first year. The year was over now and it was all set to be an amazing summer.

I spent most of my evenings during the holidays on MSN when I was indoors. I didn't really talk to strangers unless we were introduced through a group chat or something with mutual friends in common.

My best friend at the time, Dean, had put me in a group chat on MSN which also had a girl called Becky on it. I am not sure how they knew each other. It appeared as though they were also introduced on MSN. Becky and I spoke every evening and got on really well. We exchanged phone numbers and were always in touch even when we were not behind the computer.

Becky and I spoke every night. I was 20 at the time and she was 18. We spoke about everything.

I would very much call this one a cyber-relationship. It's quite scary to think that this was possible, but I very much enjoyed it as I am sure she did.

The next part is pretty crazy. After talking regularly online for a few months including exchanging a few pictures, we decided to be boyfriend and girlfriend. This was kind of insane; actually, it was extremely crazy and we were like proper teenagers again.

We even pledged to stay loyal to each other in our internet relationship. From my point of view as I had never really had a girlfriend at this point, I felt like there was no harm in us having that. I had seen pictures of her and I was like "okay if I have to be her boyfriend to tap that, then I will." I wouldn't recommend this approach to anyone because it usually ends badly. We continued our online relationship and it was going really well.

One evening during the week, Becky sent me a photo of her ass in these amazing light blue knickers. This was it for me - the point of no return. I had to tap that, one way or the other.

I spent probably about three weeks convincing Becky to agree to have me come up to Liverpool in my plan to "tap that ass." I was also gaining a general attraction for her. We got on really well and it actually felt like we were in a relationship.

Becky and I spoke about a lot of things. The very final straw came when she sent me another picture of her ass in the blue floral French knickers. On the same day in a different conversation, she mentioned she once made a guy cum in his trousers in a club from grinding. I did not think that was physically possible, but oh well. I was a 20-year-old looking to experience shit and have a great fucking time with as many beautiful women as I possibly could.

Again, I repeated "I just have to tap that." I bought a one-way national express coach ticket to Liverpool and I got on the five-hour coach one Friday night in July from Victoria coach station in London. If this was America, I would have been getting on a Greyhound coach.

It would be perfect to describe me at that point as a horny dog that was discovering himself and learning about his own sexuality along with fellow females who were in a similar situation. My destination was Liverpool, and a place called Birkenhead to be precise. I had never heard of this place or knew what it was like.

I arrived at about 12:05 am on Saturday morning and my hostess was waiting eagerly for me at the destination. She was waiting with a friend, a girl called Sara. This was the right and safe thing to do as she had never met me physically before.

All three of us were excited and cautious at the same time. For me, I was like where the fuck am I. The surroundings were not great and even though it was in the middle of the night, I could tell that I was in a pretty run-down part of the country.

Well, I was there for a reason and I told myself to stay focused on the task ahead. We walked in the scary darkness of this Liverpool suburb. I had made a room reservation at a bed and breakfast called the Black Lions Guest House. The walk lasted about ten minutes, and in that time I had done enough to convince Sara that Becky would be safe with me.

It's actually quite fascinating the things young people get up to. I was a 20-year-old and she was an 18-year-old girl. We had never met before; we randomly were on the same MSN group chat. We got introduced by someone else though, and I gathered that my friend Dean who gave the cyber introduction had not even met her yet and also had been introduced to her in the same way I had been.

I somehow managed to turn that virtual relationship into a reality. I do have skills like that, and I have been asked several times to write a book on how to get laid or find love on Tinder, Bumble, Badoo, Inner Circle and all the endless dating apps we have in our world today.

So Sara left Becky with me and we checked into the BnB. The room we had was perfect; it actually had two twin double beds. There you go. I was clever; I had booked a room with two twin beds to basically say to her "we don't have to sleep together" even though in my head it was more like "I didn't fucking come five hours on the coach to chill talk or get to know you."

Again, that's the macho guy talk coming out. If I think back, I was actually excited to be finally there with her and in actual fact, I wanted to impress her as you do when you meet a new girl.

We ordered a late Chinese takeaway and a bottle of wine from the bed and breakfast bar. We ate and drank wine until around three in the morning. I then proceeded to make my first move. By this point, I had changed my clothes and put in the prolific grey tracksuit bottoms. I went in for the kiss, and she obliged. It was an amazing kiss after months of virtual "xxx" on MSN.

This was turning out to be a good weekend already for me. After the kiss, I think I could have gone straight in but I played it cool. We had done a bit of touching and literally broke down any walls of shyness and it was clear we were going to have sex. Knowing this, I went back to eating my Chinese pork balls and dipping them in sweet and sour sauce, with the confidence that I was about to go balls-deep into Becky.

We had sex well into the early hours of Saturday morning. That whole weekend was spent eating, drinking and having sex. We did speak a bit to try and get to know each other some more. I must say, however, the hype and anticipation I had in my head was more than the real thing and I didn't really see myself ending up with her in any way. There was also the distance issue. This was basically a fantasy created online by both of us. The reality was not quite as good.

ROW 8

MY FIRST VIRGIN

JULY 2006

I had gone back to my summer job of fundraising for charity on the streets. I had chosen to be posted back in Belfast as I liked it there. It was like the return of the king. I had spent something like a month the previous year there and was becoming somewhat a celebrity. I made friends on the streets, in the pubs, and in the clubs. I even went on dates with girls I had met the previous year. This return was going to be great - the second coming of Rex to Belfast.

I remember seeing a girl pretty much catwalk towards me. She was gorgeous and made my whole face drop, not just my jaw. Well, this girl was called Victoria and I eventually stopped her and had a chat with her. We went on a date together, but I think I became too pushy as I was trying to get laid that night and I failed woefully. This Victoria never made it to Sexcellence.xlsx.

On the back of this massive fail, I shrugged my shoulders and got on with it. I was always a fan of the numbers game in the earlier part of my dating career. It always appeared that I was good at chatting girls up or had some sort of special talent. However, I totally disagree.

What I was good at was engaging large numbers of girls. For example, I would message ten girls on a Sunday asking to meet up that week. Most of the time I used a generic copy and paste message. This might have resulted in two wrong numbers and two girls who changed their minds, so I would be left with six.

To meet up with a girl, you need to engage her and give her a reason to meet you. In our world, or in my world ten years ago, getting the number was the easy part. She wasn't just going to say "follow me on Insta" or "add me on Snapchat." It was phone number or nothing. This allowed me to fill up my phonebook quickly.

When you message a girl at the start, the conversation needs to be smooth and flow and not seem forced. You need to get a few laughs, a few questions from her, and also you should always try and wind her up about something. These three guidelines are key.

Well, I am not trying to replicate the book "The Game" here so enough with the tips. Let us get back to the spreadsheet. The next potential entry could have been one of six girls. It ended up being a girl called Nicole who I actually met in Bangor. This was a coastal town in Northern Ireland which had a beach.

My job placed me on the very hilly high street which meant I was very visible and approachable. In Bangor, I actually played a part in a TV show for the BBC called 'Just for Laughs.' Apparently, I acted well. I never got to watch the show myself but I got told about it when I went back to university.

So let us get talking about Nicole. Do you remember Lucy? Similar story apart from the fact that I signed her up herself to donate monthly to the charity I was working for. It's a funny one. I signed her up and then she asked who my colleague was. He was a guy called Mike, a tall good looking Goth with several tattoos and piercings.

I said "His name is Mike; let me introduce you." So I called Mike over and he came and said hi, and they flirted a bit back and forth. I laughed along and helped them flirt with each other. Haha why not? Rex can't have everyone he wants.

Well on this particular occasion I could. So, weirdly, Mike went off and I asked Nicole for her number and said I'd get Mike to message her. In the car on the drive back to Belfast, I think I messaged her first and I kept talking about Mike and setting them up.

By the time I got back to Belfast I think she had somehow hit her head and she then switched from fancying Mike to fancying me. I mentioned it to him out of respect. Ideally, I would just stay clear. In this case, he had only actually spoken to Nicole for maybe ten minutes, so she wasn't quite his. I still asked to be polite anyway.

He gave me the go-ahead and so I invited her to the house in Belfast. Different house from Lucy as this was the following year. She arrived in a taxi and we walked over to the supermarket to buy drinks. We had quite a few drinks and then it was time for sex. Well, she said that. So she then told me she had only ever been fingered before but she had never had sex. She was a Virgin. I had to do this one carefully to keep her at ease - Rex with the softest of touches in every way.

I was learning; I was really learning as a man to hone my sexual skills and tailor them based on the requirements of my partner. So I was very nice and tender with her. It took maybe half hour to put it in. But once it was in, she loved it and begged me not to stop. To be honest I wasn't the exact sex pro myself. Remember? At the end she wanted me to cum on her tits. Now that's pretty easy for me to control and aim.

On that particular occasion I had never had any specialised or tailored cumming instructions from a girl, so when I felt it coming, I whipped my cock out, tried to aim for her tits and literally missed and completely sprayed the wall behind her. It was like firing eight darts at a dartboard and all of them ending up on the wall. I said to myself, "Rex you have a lot to learn mate."

On the whole, Nicole and I enjoyed the time we spent together; she takes the title of the first virgin on my spreadsheet. Well, the only one.... so far. I was in Northern Ireland for another couple of weeks so we were not able to establish or maintain a relationship.

However, I did take off the ring on my pinkie finger and give it to her as a gift as I was extremely proud to share this first experience with her.

ROW 9

I SHAGGED MY COLLEAGUE

JULY 2006

It was still in the summer. I had spent eight weeks in Northern Ireland working as a charity fundraiser on the streets. A very eventful eight weeks, in which I shared a very special moment with Nicole by being part of her first sexual experience.

Another special moment was witnessing a close colleague of mine turn vegetarian. James was my team leader and we bonded very well over a spliff or two that summer. Whenever I wasn't going on dates or clubbing in the evenings after work, we would chill out together.

One evening when we were staying in a farmhouse outside of Lisburn, we lit up a spliff and watched the cows. He got so caught up with them while high and decided they were too cute to be eaten and so he decided to go vegetarian. I understand he hasn't switched back even today.

Two great moments that summer and I was about to have a third. Let's see how special the next girl on the spreadsheet is. Helen from Manchester, a 29-year-old cute brunette as you can see from her row on the spreadsheet. At this point, I had only been with brunettes. This was not out of preference; I just kept taking what I got as most guys do at some point in their lives, if not for their whole lives.

Helen was the new starter in our team, and for her first week, we were posted to a small town called Witney near Oxford. Our house was on a quiet street. But luckily we had a pub across the street from us.

We had arrived in Witney on Sunday and I had arrived in Helen by Thursday. When she joined the team, I must confess I didn't particularly find her attractive. She was okay looking though I guess. Perhaps the fact that I didn't appear too keen on her in a sense made me more attractive, combined with the fact that I had a reputation amongst my team members of being a womaniser.

It's so strange how such a "false" reputation added value to me and made my life easier. Yes "false," in the sense that I was extremely inexperienced and very new to the dating and sex games. I was far from a womaniser; I was just very keen at exploring relationships with the opposite sex. But I did to a certain extent use that "womaniser" tag to my advantage and I definitely played on it very well.

So on Thursday night, I went to the pub with my team. We all had a few beers and were definitely very merry. I was feeling drunk, and so was Helen. We both got into having a good chat and conversation as well as a good laugh. Eventually, everyone left her and me in the pub and they all went home and to bed. We stayed chatting and joking around until midnight when the pub shut.

We then walked across the road to the house. At that point, I literally had zero intentions. She was my colleague and I wasn't one to try it on with my colleagues. I am very much a believer of the phrase "don't shit where you eat." But you will find that I did contradict this on more than one occasion, with devastating consequences for that matter as you will find out later in this book as you read on.

Well, so there I was, 20-year-old Rex sitting on the couch with 29-year-old Helen. The lights in the living room were dim and everyone was asleep.

She turned the TV on and had it on a low volume. Still, there were no dirty thoughts in my mind. Ha ha... I know you wouldn't believe that. But believe me, I had no such intentions. I left her on the couch and went downstairs to change into casual clothes. Yes, the grey Nike track pants came on, and a white T-shirt. This literally became my sex uniform. I got changed and went back up and took my place next to her on the couch.

We spoke a bit more and then "the magic happened." Well, you will need to read a bit more as we didn't have sex at this point. What happened was magical to me though. I had an erection despite not having any sexual thoughts that I remember, and she randomly felt it and that just got her wild.

She said she had never felt anything so hard and that was there a metal rod under there. She checked to see what the rod was and it was just my hard cock. She dived in head first and sucked me off in a Claire-esque way. Until this point, Claire the American Amy-Lee lookalike had given me the best blow job ever. This was decent too. She sucked and sucked until I couldn't hold it anymore and I came in her mouth. We then went to bed.

24 hours later on Friday night, my other colleagues David and Lauren joined us for a kitchen spliff as our nightcap. All four of us smoked and chatted. It was strange as I had kind of fancied Lauren all along as she had been on my team during those eight weeks in Northern Ireland and she knew what I was like.

Anyway, so we had the spliff and Helen tapped me and asked me to come with her downstairs. She dragged me to my bedroom, locked the door, and started sucking my dick again.

I made it to my bag, reached for a condom and fucked her. She then rode me until I came. During this time, Lauren came and knocked on the door. We stayed silent and then she ran back up the stairs in excitement as if ready to tell our other colleagues what her suspicions were.

The sex with Helen was ok; I don't remember it being that spectacular. But I was learning that sex isn't always amazing with everyone. It's like a formula with a whole lot of variables for it to work.

I spent one more night in Oxford and that was my last day on that job as I was heading back to university again. I had also had two good summers on the job and felt like I had done my time. Helen and I texted each other a couple of times over the next month or so until everything eventually fizzled out and we didn't speak again.

ROW 10

THE DANCEFLOOR CREEP

SEPTEMBER 2006

It was the first day back at university and I had completed one year where I had my fair share of pussy for a fresher or a freshman. It was time to build on that whilst growing as a man.

I must say, I always did look to find a girl who I would love and share a relationship with. For some reason, I couldn't get that. I was better at getting laid than having a relationship with a girl. I guess it was just the lion mentality I had. It was more about building my numbers up than getting on the romantic level with a girl.

There was a girl I did fancy at the time, but I think she had heard too many bad things about me to consider having anything serious. I tried so many things to convince her. I even took her to a Hillsong Church in London to try and make her understand that I was boyfriend material. This was hilarious being I was the same guy who had all these amateur sex tapes floating around campus being shared by Bluetooth.

It was the second year and I was definitely a bit more mature. I had gotten dropped off in my new apartment by my mum. I went in and dropped my stuff and headed to one of the university bars.

Whilst there I gathered that several of the freshers were headed to a bar called Walkabout at Temple in London. Three or four snakebites later, I threw up and was back up and ready to head out. Snakebite was a very popular drink back then. It was a deadly mix of beer, cider, and blackcurrant. Deadly as fuck but it got you smashed pretty quickly.

I was definitely ready for the night and also to pick up where I started from the previous year. Rex was back. I was even more confident than the previous year.

I had worked all summer so I had a bit of money in my pocket; I was no more a teen, getting older, going to the gym, had more facial hair, was getting taller. This was me developing all the physical features as well as sharpening up my game to become one of the most prolific non-celebrity bachelors London has ever seen.

On this particular night, I was hanging out with a group of four friends. We were messing around on the dancefloor as always. At some point in the night I made eye contact with a girl.

She was in a group with three guys and another girl. I remember making eye contact with her more than once. I carried on with my night, and I noticed she was creeping closer and closer. It was like something out of 'Macbeth' where she was 'Birnam Wood' and I was

'Dunsinane Hill'. If you have not read that, I do recommend you do as well as a few of my other Shakespearean favourites like Hamlet, and of course 'Romeo and Juliet'.

So, it turns out the girl's name was Kelly. She had crept over fully and was dancing right behind me. This could not be more obvious. I took the opportunity and spoke to her. She was in the year above me, and a bit older.

We walked back to her place with her housemates, three guys and one girl. They were teasing her that I was younger. I had to overcome this challenge and stay calm and mature whilst walking with my arm around her waist. Basically saying "I am young, but I can protect you".

Girls always need to feel safe with you. I know this is a basic principle, but we do forget these basic principles sometimes. It goes way back to ancient times when the strongest warriors got the best women. Well, so I made Kelly feel safe and comfortable with me.

When we got back to hers, we went straight to her room. I sat on the bed and she offered me a glass of water. She sat next to me and all of a sudden we went from "0-100 real quick". First she went from kissing me to sucking my dick and then stripping fully whilst my clothes were still on. It was amazing and hilarious. I had to play catch-up with the stripping.

I fucked her for ages all night. I think we had four hours sleep or so. We woke up and had more sex. It was great sex. I left as soon as the tank felt empty and I couldn't carry on anymore. She was also pretty sore too. That was an amazing night with Kelly and she fully deserved her place on my spreadsheet.

So far 99% of the girls I had slept with were older than me. This was becoming a trend. Well, I must say, the older girls did prepare me for the several 18-25 year old girls I was about to meet, fall in love with or shag over the next ten years.

ROW 11

WHY DID I DO IT?

SEPTEMBER 2006

It was the first week of term at university. I had shagged Kelly from a bar called Walkabout on my first night back. I was buzzing with excitement and feeling confident about every night out. There were new faces around - the freshers or freshmen as they are called from across the pond.

Being the first week, there was the usual non-stop drinking before we got down to actual work and academics. I had taken the bus to campus on one of the days to get some registration sorted out. On my way there, whilst with a friend, I saw a girl who sat facing me on the bus.

It was at the rear of one of those double-decker London buses where you have four seats and the front two are facing the back two. So this girl sat across from me and smiled. She was bold and even introduced herself and got involved in our conversation.

Actually, I'm mistaken. My friend John and I were talking about something. I am not sure exactly what we were talking about but I somehow asked for her opinion. So actually I was the bold one, brewing with the confidence of a thoroughbred stallion who had won back to back Grand National titles.

By the way, Grand National is a major horseracing event which takes place in the UK every year. I would have been able to talk more about that as I nearly shagged a winning jockey's daughter in Brighton a few years ago.

Let's switch back to the bus. Picture it: confident guy, talking loud on the bus and getting girls involved in the conversation. I was appealing to anyone watching. So, we got off the bus and I forgot about the girl I met. I didn't even know her name and I didn't even ask for it or for any contact details.

Fast forward one week later on a Sunday evening. This was now two Sundays after I had fucked Kelly. I got a text from a friend on my course Alex saying he met a girl who knows me and fancies me. I was thinking what is this "manna from heaven" situation? So I went along with it.

I then remembered the girl from the bus and it was her. Her name was Natasha. She had obviously found me very attractive on that bus ride. I must say, however, she seemed nice but I didn't find her attractive at all. This was becoming an Anna-like situation.

I can't explain it but there's something about us young men which means we are able to sleep with girls even though we don't really find them attractive. It's like isolating the pussy. It's like imagining the pussy is a separate entity from the person or their emotions. We are able to separate these different parts of a female into these two entities, the pussy and the person.

Let me pause for a second and explain this a bit more with examples. There have been times in my life when I feel horny, and at that point, my thought process is controlled by my dick. Yes, the dick becomes responsible for the majority of my actions and thoughts while in this horny state. I could start to get into conversations with girls, and my dick would convince me that I liked this girl or that girl, and I would continue to flirt with her and message her and even try to meet up.

Let's say I paused for a moment and had a wank while feeling like this. At this point, I lose interest in messaging or meeting up with that girl. I always say, if you still think about a girl the moment after you cum from a wank, that girl is the girl you should date.

Anyway, back to Natasha from the spreadsheet; so she fancied me. She told a mutual friend and I passed my number to her through him. We then began texting, and then after a few texts back and forth, we arranged to meet up on a Sunday again. This was a Sunday fling without planning it.

When that Sunday evening came, I took the bus down to her dorm which was about 15 minutes away. I got in there and she made me a drink of vodka and coke.

Well, that pretty much would have spelled out her intentions I guess. Basically meaning "Rex, I intend to get you smashed and absolutely fuck the shit out of you."

You see now it's the other way around; it's the girl doing to me what I had done to other girls. This is why I see my spreadsheet as a celebration of these girls and I feel privileged sharing some great and some not so great moments with each and every one of them.

Natasha put on the movie "Blood Diamond." It featured my favourite actor Leonardo DiCaprio, so I was excited. I didn't fancy the girl that much but there was vodka and my favourite actor. She made the effort so she deserved the smash. We watched the movie and she started sharing with me how she came from wealth, and how she spent time in Africa on a gap year. She definitely had a great personality.

So let's get straight to the point. Eventually, we kissed and then we started fucking. She went on top of me and then me on top of her and then we switched to doggy style. Again I wasn't so attracted to her but I was still sleeping with her. It's almost like I felt I was doing her a favour.

But why? Why did I need to put myself through this if there was no benefit? I couldn't even use bragging rights as most of my friends didn't find her that attractive. So, what was the reason? And why do men do this even today? I will share more experiences like this later on in the book and hopefully when you read the whole book you can make your own conclusions about why men do this.

So the worst part of this row on the spreadsheet was that I was struggling to cum during sex with Natasha. So, I got my phone out and put on the video of me fucking Anita. I was then watching that video while Natasha rode me. This might have been the rudest thing I had ever done in my life. This deeply upset her and that was the end of the sex. She kicked me out.

I literally nearly forgot my cock inside her pussy. She just kicked me out of her pussy and her flat. I don't think I need to explain why I had no future with Natasha. But I surely did learn a thing or two about what not to do when sleeping with a girl.

ROW 12

MY FIRST TRUE LOVE

OCTOBER 2006

So it was maybe four weeks into term-time and my 21st birthday was coming up. I was still kind of recovering and telling myself off for how I handled the whole Natasha situation. My birthday is on 1st of November and so it usually coincides with all the Halloween parties.

There was a huge one coming up at the Ministry of Sound Nightclub in London. This was on the 31st of October and it was the perfect setting to ring in my 21st. I even had multiple tickets bought for me by friends to attend this party.

So Halloween, I think I had been kind of fed up of fancy dress and wasn't feeling like dressing up on the night. I think my thought process went like "what girl would sleep with me when I have this face paint, fangs, cape and mask on. Well obviously there are fetish people who like that stuff, but I didn't know of any.

Hence, against Halloween spirit, I decided to put on a white shirt and some jeans. I stood out like a sore thumb in the club. So we were all in there all taking pictures. Most people were dressed up and there were some pretty cool outfits if I remember right. I kind of wished I was dressed up at this point.

Fast forward a couple of hours into the night. It was about 11:30 or so and my friend John comes over to me on the dancefloor and asks to come with him to meet a friend on his course called Thierry. I said ok and I went over with him.

We went to the bar in the next room and there was a group of about three guys and four girls who were housemates. I said hello to them. There was a blonde girl called Louise in the group. We spoke a bit, she seemed interested in me. It was probably fifteen minutes to my 21st birthday, so I decided to stay around talking to her until the clock struck midnight. Maybe I would have got a 'birthday kiss' because once again a kiss is the gateway drug as we know. The gateway drug to sex.

So, I was hoping for some birthday sex also. So, I hung out with this group, and we drank and danced all night. I left the club with Louise and her friends and we headed back. Luckily they lived not too far away from me and so we all jumped in one large taxi. They got dropped off first.

When we got off I kind of knew I wasn't going to get anything that night. Louise had rejected my kiss earlier in the club. So I had two options. Try for the kiss again or play it cool like it doesn't matter. I went for the latter option. I think this definitely paid off. We parted ways

that night. No birthday kiss and no birthday sex. "Pffff...
I was disappointed but I had met a girl who seemed
really nice and who also had an amazing body with one
of the best butts I had ever seen.

People often ask me whether I prefer breasts or bums.
And I say "don't forget the legs". I do go through phases
and moods where I prefer one over the other. Overall
though, I think I prefer bums, to legs to boobs in that
order.

So Louise had an amazing bum and I was gutted I
wasn't able to explore it a bit more on that occasion.
Anyone who knows me would know I have the
stickability and Persistence when it comes to women I
like. The spreadsheet would probably have been only
10 or 20 rows long if not for these qualities.

A few days later, we agreed to meet up. I then found
out that the issue was that she had a boyfriend. An
older one, about 8 years older than me. He could
obviously offer way more for her in every way. I was just
this kid who was discovering life.

My approach to this was to kind of talk about the little
things I would like to do with her. Things her boyfriend
maybe might have overlooked and basically make her
feel like she would have much more fun with me. For
example, I asked her if she smoked weed. She said that
she had not had it in a while as her boyfriend did not
like it. I then said I was going to have a spliff that night

but that she could stay next to me while I had it. We ended up having a spliff together.

I made her feel young and alive again. Having a much older boyfriend made her stop doing some of the things she would have liked.

Straight after the spliff, which we smoked on a park bench near her house, she invited me back to hers. Boom! I was in. We proceeded to have sex. It was great and memorable. This lead to a rollercoaster ride with Louise as she still had a boyfriend. She proceeded to end things with him.

I ended up receiving several threats from her boyfriend but I stood above it all. Rex was a born winner, and obviously this was not a game. I had won a heart. My relationship Louise ended up being the longest relationship I had ever had. We were together for five years.

ROW 13

THE EASY REBOUND

JUNE 2012

I had broken up with my girlfriend of five years Louise. The main reason for the break up was due to the fact that she wanted more. She wanted to take things to the next stage by perhaps getting married and having kids. It wasn't something I was ready for as I was only about 26 at the time. I had got a job in finance and had been living with a friend in a shared central London apartment after university.

At this point, if I thought I had lived life. Well, I had not seen anything yet. I was about to start living "that life" full on. The life of an eligible bachelor. My flatmate Alex had an Italian girlfriend. Her name was Daniella. Naturally, we always went out together, me him and her friends.

On one occasion, her friend Sophie came out with us one night. We all went to a bar in Camden called Proud on a Friday night. I had been complacent in the past when I have been set up with girls by friends. I assumed that because we were being set up it was a done deal. But in actual fact I think it's harder. It leads to a battle of minds.

The girl thinks that you think you are guaranteed to have her. So, she would then try to prove to you that nothing is guaranteed. She doesn't want to come across as "easy". So, I would suggest that when we are being set up, we can show interest at the start, then gradually wane out interest. Mess with her head. Give her attention and then take it back for half of the same amount of time if she seems to be responding well to the attention. For example, give her attention for an hour. Take it back for 30 minutes and continue the cycle.

Girls do the same to us all the time without meaning it and this ideology and mentality has helped me bed several girls. This seemed to be working with Sophie.

We partied all night at Proud with lots of drinks and shots. We were all having a great time. I remember the defining moment was getting Sophie to come back with me. I had kissed her on the dance floor. Also as my friend Alex was coming back to our flat with his girlfriend Daniella, it was quite likely that Sophie would come back. I obviously played it cool and didn't really ask her, I kind of just let things happen as I still didn't want to show complacency by assuming she was coming back with us.

Eventually, we got in a taxi back to our place. So, it was basically two couples, Alex and Daniella were the horniest couple ever and they used to have the wildest loudest sex.

I was back at our place with Sophie, and we could hear them having sex a few minutes after we got back. I said to Sophie, "you could sleep in my bed while I sleep on the couch". I said it with a non-presumptuous straight innocent face. This was a humorous part of my ploy to bed her. I pretended to be oblivious to the possibility that we were both going to have sex that night.

You know what though, we eventually were laying in my bed and I still had to convince her that I had fancied her for a while. This was a lie. I don't really know how other guys do it but I will be honest with you. I have bedded a lot of girls by saying things like this. It is probably my main technique. I wouldn't call it a lie though because I am usually attracted to the girls in a physical way at the least. But I do exaggerate by saying I "fancy' them in order to bed them.

I eventually convinced her to take her clothes off so we could have a naked cuddle. My best memory of that night ended up with her getting so horny and riding me and fucking me with her 32DD natural girl breasts bouncing up and down.

It was a very memorable night, and I appreciated every single moment of it. This was literally like a mutual one-night stand. For her, she had heard of me previously and it seemed like a pleasure she was happy enough with to have that one night with me.

ROW 14

GETTING BACK IN THE GAME

JULY 2012

I was full on single now and in the full swing of single life. I had gone out with one of my friends Gary to a bar called Kelly's. It was a bar with two floors with mainly commercial and chart music playing. Even though I had finished University, I still spent the next few years after that revisiting similar bars and clubs that I was used to while I was a student.

We were in this bar which became a club after 11pm or so. I remember a girl looking at me constantly. She looked on the dance floor and I smiled and went over to her. She was with a friend and I was with a friend too. It was a natural "2 on 2" pairing. Her friend was not the most attractive girl around but I do respect my buddy for still being my wingman and talking to her friend while I tested out "my game" on this girl. To be honest I had seen him do worse up till then so by his standards she was probably ok.

This is what makes the world go round you know. We all like different types of people. I certainly am not everyone's cup of tea at first glance, as with most people. But I can stand up and show you that I made the most of what I can get.

I would like to use this to inspire all the guys and girls out there. Tall, short, small, big, and whatever shade of the colour spectrum you are. There is someone out there who will appreciate you. You just need to get them to think about you. This is the challenging bit. Be confident, play the game.

I hope that by the time you are done reading this book I would be able to have subtly passed on my mentality and mindset on how I dealt with different challenges in different dating scenarios and turned them into sex or love.

We spent the night dancing with Stacey and her friend and eventually, as they were pretty keen and young. They were both 18. I remember making sure of this by looking at their driving licenses. We were able to make suggestions and take control of the situation. I suggested they came back to mine.

We all got in a taxi and went back to my place. This was pretty calm and clinical. Both girls wanted to get laid.

I like the fact I am sharing this particular spreadsheet entry with you. It was one of those that were pretty easy to execute. I feel like the girls had made their minds up that "as long as these guys were nice to us and safe," they were going to sleep with us. It was a matter of getting back home, going into my room and getting into bed.

I got into bed with Stacey and we spoke for a little bit and then had sex. We had so much fun together that we woke up in the morning and played PlayStation also. That was a classic fun night. Another mutual one-night stand for the spreadsheet.

ROW 15

WORKING THE BACKLOG

JULY 2012

I was getting older, more experienced, more confident, more attractive and attracting girls from different backgrounds.

I must say it helped that I had a long-term relationship previously. That always sounded more appealing to girls in the sense that they always saw me more like "boyfriend potential" because of that. Obviously, I always continued to play on this and use it to my advantage. Even if I had decided when I met a girl that I probably might not want to have anything more than sex with her I still continued to give that impression. This was what worked for me.

Men should find what works for them without changing too much of whom they are. For me, I was a nice gentleman who had a promiscuous past. I found that this was extremely appealing to girls. They found it exciting; they loved knowing I had a mysterious past. I think it even got them wet. Girls would have to answer why themselves as I don't have an answer to that theory from a girl's point of view.

I lived most of my sexual life with this mentality. Obviously, if you have read the book from the beginning, you know how this started with the sex tapes and the whole reputation I started off with at University.

From my university days, I was pretty popular and very social. I did have a sort of backlog of girls who I knew that I would like to maybe be with if I was single. I was now single so I decided to explore one or two of these avenues.

The exploration led to the first "Doctor" on the spreadsheet, a girl called Harriet. She was from a small village in Wales and she had an amazing accent which I fell in love with when I had heard her speak back at Uni. She was still studying and was training to be a doctor. I had agreed to catch up with a bunch of university mates and we had planned to go to the same student club that Harriet was going to be at one night.

I arrived at the club with two friends, Alex and James. James was a David Beckham lookalike and got a lot of attention from the ladies. Naturally, Alex and I fed on the scraps. However, I didn't need to feed on scraps on this occasion. Harriet was so happy to see me, and we spoke and caught up on what I had been up to since university.

We had an intellectual conversation about her course also. She was about to go into specialist training to be a gynaecologist. I thought to myself "if I bed you tonight we might need some gynaecologist assistance because I'm going to be pumping you so hard we might make some babies."

We danced and drank and we were all really smashed. I remember trying for two hours to kiss her. She was having none of it. Three or four jaeger-bombs later, she kissed me. I was too drunk to feel that excited. But it was great. I remember she was totally in control of what we did. I remember giving up on sleeping with her on that night. I just stopped thinking about it.

But then when the club shut, she came over, grabbed me, straight to the cloakroom and she was like "Let's go back to yours". I played it cool and was like sure, let's head up and get a cab. Obviously, in my head it was more like "ok let's fucking go right now, I'll give you a piggyback home if I could".

My friends were so impressed; I remember James was even jealous when he saw me jump in a cab with her. The hot young doctor was about to get fucked by Rex. We got in a cab back to mine.

We got to my place, everything was looking great. She stripped naked, got in my bed and fell asleep. She was obviously pretty drunk. There was no sex for me that night. I was drunk myself, so I stayed patient and I fell asleep next to a naked girl who I wanted to sleep with. This was like torture.

I woke up in the middle of the night and cuddled her with my hard on. She then woke up and we started kissing. I was then able to slide it in and fuck her while spooning. What a win for me. I had long wanted to fuck Harriet, her lips, eyes and amazing tanned legs always got me every time. This was a major victory for me and the second experience of welsh seduction on my spreadsheet.

I did see Harriet a couple of times over the next couple of months and we did sleep together again. It all fizzled out naturally though as I think this was purely lust from my point of view.

ROW 16

COMPLACENT REX

AUGUST 2012

It was the summer of 2012 and I still had this backlog of girls I had met at university and had not really met up with or anything. There was one particular one called Elan. She was tall, blonde and Irish. She had massive boobs also. I didn't realize how nice her boobs were until I actually met up with her, to be honest, I say she was on a backlog. She wasn't really on any strategic list. She wasn't even on my phone or in my mind. However, she came into both on a night out.

I was at an 80s night at a bar called Reflex in London when I bumped into her. She was playing hard to get and all that as we always used to kind of look at each other back at university. I spoke to her for a bit and then we managed to exchange numbers. I did try a bit harder that night but it was to no avail. Perhaps she could see that I was pretty desperate to smash her.

Having her number was good enough because I must say I lost my composure that night. I was utterly crap. All my principles and fundamentals went out of the window. I went full on aggressive talking to her for too long. Being all touchy feely too soon etc. It's like I assumed I was going to smash her. That was just a terrible performance. Maybe the 80s music and cheap shots and 80s colourful dancefloor with bright lights got into my head.

Anyway, the best thing I did on this night was to get her number. So much work on text was required. She didn't exactly play hard to get or anything. I was just shit. Ha ha... Eventually, we agreed to meet up. And guess what our meet up was. It was for me to go to her place directly to watch a movie and chill.

It was like university days again when your first dates were in bedrooms. Gone are those days. No need to book a restaurant, no need to buy drinks and food and all that. I jumped at the opportunity to go back to hers.

She was a practicing nurse in London. I was kind of hoping she was working that day and maybe if I got there earlier she would be in her work outfit. Haha... bringing those fantasies to a reality. I bet all my male readers love that.

I arrived at her place. It was a shared house in South London. I walked in and she introduced me to her housemate Sarah. Again these fantasies just never happen. Elan wasn't wearing her nursing outfit, and there was no suggestion or hint of a threesome with Sarah. "Come off it Rex".

The number of times I have wished fantasies came true. I guess that came up from watching porn parodies as a teenager long before I ever set my eyes, fingers or tongue on a pussy.

On this particular evening, I received the tease of my life. Elan was wearing a baggy tee shirt and short shorts. I sat in one end of her bed and she sat on the other.

I usually stand so far away from a girl when we get into that sort of situation early on. Also when I bring a girl back from a night out and I am not certain we would have sex I stand back for a moment and chat. Obviously, I would be different if she was up for fucking straight away. If you want to test that, just kiss her passionately and put your hands in certain places. You will be able to tell by her reaction what she wants, or at least how far you are likely to be able to go with her on that occasion.

So we sat far apart... I didn't bother apologising for how full on I was on her when I bumped into her out. You know what, it fucking worked cos here I was about to smash her. Well was I though? You will find out shortly.

You would think she is on the spreadsheet for a reason though right? She did something; she bent over forward facing me. "Oh my God". My jaw dropped. Her boobies were amazing and huge and she was proud to flaunt them. I usually am an ass and legs man but I do appreciate very much a nice pair of juicy tits. Elan had these. At this moment I just wanted to suck them. I would have been happy to suck them and head home.

So we sat and talked and watched some TV and I had a few glasses of wine.

While chatting and laughing away, I eventually had a breakthrough after like two hours of playing it cool. There is only so much of that a man can do. We can just about play it cool to the point where they start wondering "what does this guy want. Does he fancy me? But he doesn't act like it". Get them thinking. Puzzle their brains.

So I eventually kissed Elan. The first thing I fucking did whilst kissing her was to grab her boobs. I had been waiting to do that all evening. We had a nice kiss. I thought the deal was sealed. She didn't let me have sex with her that night. I stayed overnight at hers and woke up in the morning with a massive hard on. It was a long walk of shame back home with no sex.

But wait a minute, again there is a reason she made it onto the spreadsheet. Three days later, she agreed to pay me a return visit.

I got the alcohol ready. I had got the movie ready. Actually, I set this up differently. It wasn't a movie, it was the PlayStation. Some of you girls might think "what the fuck", and some might think that was cute. So instead of the stereotypical movie etc. We played a game called "little big planet".

We played the game for about an hour while we were drinking. She even suggested a drinking game. I don't remember how the rules worked but not went hand in hand with the game we were playing.

Eventually, she paused and went to the bathroom. She came back and dragged me out of the chair to my bed and started off what I was hoping would be foreplay. Nothing is ever foreplay unless it precedes sex. Remember that one.

We started kissing and I started rubbing and sucking her tits. I was sucking her nipples and then I thought of fingering her. I slipped my finger under her trousers and started fingering her clitoris at the same time with the same rhythm and frequency as I was licking her nipples. This drove her wild. She then whispered in her Irish accent. "I want you to put it inside me".

Fireworks went off all over my body. It was the moment to clap my palms together and take a run-up and land dick-first into her amazing, pretty, soft and wet pussy. I fucked Elan for about twenty minutes and then I came in her mouth at her request. I fucked her again and came on her tits at my request. This was a great achievement because she was so fucking hot in my eyes. I did fancy Elan and wanted a bit more than sex.

We kept in touch and I genuinely thought I might have had a chance of being with her. Things took a wrong turn when I went mad at her for going for dinner with her ex. I didn't actually realise she was actually trying to mend things with him. I lost my temper with her and that was the end of it. I recently heard she is now married to that ex now.

Thinking back, I definitely had a chance with her, but I didn't deal with the situation with enough maturity. It would have definitely been possible to treat her in a way that she would forget her ex in a minute and turn all her focus on me. I could probably make that happen now with my confidence and experience. You will learn more as you continue reading the book.

ROW 17

GIRLS CHEAT TOO

AUGUST2012

I had given up on any chance of getting back with Elan. I did feel sort of heartbroken as I did like her and I saw her as much more than one night of fun. Well, there was nothing I could do at this point. I had a night out planned the following weekend, so I had something to look forward to.

When the Saturday night came, I went out with a few of my friends to Fez Club in Putney. This is the first of a few mentions you will hear of his club in my book. On this occasion, I didn't actually meet a girl in the club.

However, if you ever spent time with me, or spent a night out with me and my friends, there will be two phrases you will become familiar with. One is "last chance Lucy". This is when you don't have a girl to go back home with, and you have like fifteen minutes left until the club closes. What happens is that you then drop all standards, and then literally go for any girl. I have been guilty of this once or twice.

On this particular evening, I think. I had even tried for a "last chance Lucy", I got nothing. What a fail. The second phrase you will be more familiar with. It is very cliché, but very true "it's is not over until it's over".

The night out was over and at 4am when the club shut, but then there was the kebab shop left. As we were all starving, we walked over to a kebab shop around the corner. We were in great spirits. At the end of the day, it shouldn't always be about getting with girls on nights out, but we guys have to admit that we can't help but have that on our minds most of the time.

My friend Harry and I started talking to the girls on the table behind us. At this point, it was not about chat up lines or any of that. This was drunk "kebab banter" we spoke to them while we ate and then all of a sudden, after food, there was light at the end of the kebab tunnel. The girls invited Harry and I back to their place.

There was a group of four girls. I had to choose quickly otherwise I would have made a mess of the situation. I had been in situations in the past where made a mess of a situation involving a group of girls. Although that ended up in me bedding a girl who later became famous on X-factor UK.

On this particular night, I decided to go for the blondie in the group. Her name was 'Emma' and she was a Nurse at Charing Cross hospital in London, I was clearly on a roll with Nurses. And yes she was called 'Emma' if you remember from my introduction at the start of this book. Obviously, that had nothing to do with my decision as I had not really been with many 'Emma's' until this point to be honest.

So we walked back to their place, it was in Putney and literally five minutes' walk down the road. There was no messing about. Emma took me straight back to her room. I started kissing her, and like within a minute we were having sex. It's crazy, the time-span from the kebab to the bed was probably about 35 minutes. Well so I started having sex with her and we did it for about ten minutes and then I came.

I was thinking to myself "Okay Rex, ten minutes rest and then slip it in again". But that was not going to happen. Emma suddenly started crying and saying "you have to go, you have to go". She was crying profusely saying she can't believe she has just cheated on her boyfriend. I was like "err... oops". What do you even say to that?

I think I said "Well... I'm sorry and you're a lovely girl". I had no idea what to say. It was one of my weirdest sexual experiences ever. I tried to kiss and hug her. She was having none of it and she literally kicked me out.

I put my clothes back on as quickly as possible and I was out on the street in a couple of minutes. I found it weird that she could be so responsive during sex and then right after it suddenly clicked in her head what she had done. I might need a girl to explain this to me as I struggled to understand what had gone on.

This was inevitably a one-night stand, maybe not even that. I would just call it "a quick shag with a stranger ". I truly hoped after that Emma would have tried to put that behind her. Whether it was confessing what she did to her boyfriend, for the sake of honesty or just completely forgetting about it and acting like it never happened. Either way, for me it was an eye-opener and proof that girls also cheat in the way that guys do.

ROW 18

DOGGING ON THE BEACH

AUGUST 2012

I was having a fairly good month of August. It was now time for a summer break. A few of my mates. Well, I say a few, there were around ten of us who jetted off to the island of Mallorca in Spain for a nice week long holiday. The holiday was going very well, and we had got tickets on one of the biggest DJs in the world, Avicii. It was all set to be a good night. We had pre-drinks in our hotel room after doing 100m sprints in the corridor. Yes, boys will be boys.

We then headed out to an outdoor square outside the live venue where we had a few more drinks. In this square, we met a bunch of girls who were also from England as is the case on most Spanish islands.

I invited the girls over to our little standing table in the corner of the square. We all downed shots of tequila together. We also drank something purple out of some plastic purple tower which was full of ice and a purple drink. I have no idea what the drink was, but believe me it got us all fucking smashed.

I know that from what you have read so far, I do come across as an extremely confident guy who approaches any girl he wants. I become even more confident with alcohol in my system as you can imagine. There is nothing wrong with that, confidence is the key here. I would say to every guy, do whatever it is that works for you to make you feel the most confident you can be.

Remember I was part of a group of ten guys; eight of the guys went into the club where Avicii was playing. My friend Ed and I stayed with the girls. One of them had caught Ed's eye, and of course, I also had my pick in the group. Her name was Lizzie. She was a tall brunette from Essex, England.

Essex is a county right next to London on the North/East side. The rest of Lizzie's group was also from Essex. There are a lot of blogs and articles and Reality TV shows on Essex girls. So I will not go into details on stereotypes, but I will let any unfamiliar readers go and do your research on that.

After a few more drinks, we decided to go into the club where Avicii was playing, after all we had tickets for it. But then the girls did not have tickets. So we only went into the part of the venue where tickets were not required. Avicii was not playing in this part and he could not be seen or heard. We had basically sacrificed our €80 tickets for the possibility of getting some pussy. There was no guarantee here, but we knew it might be worth the gamble. Plus, the dick brain was in control here. Yes, the dick brain. Trust me it truly exists.

We stayed in the venue for a few more drinks and danced a bit. The girls then suggested we go for a walk on the beach. I say "the girls'. It was just the two girls we had been chatting up. The rest of the girls in their group were nowhere to be found.

Ed and I were really up for a walk on the beach. The only sex on the beach I had ever had was the cocktail. So in my mind, I was like.. 'hmm this is going to be great'. The beach was only a ten-minute walk. On this walk were Lizzie who I was getting with and had already kissed, Hayley, who Ed was getting with and then Ed and I. We were the envy of every guy we walked past as both girls were really hot. They were also very well dressed and it looked like they had made a good effort on this night out. We were about to find out whether we would become "worthy" prizes for their efforts.

We made the leisurely walk to the beach, even stopping for a drink along the way. We got to the beach, sat on one sunbed each. Ed and Hayley ended up walking a bit further on until we were out of each other's sights.

I sat on my sunbed with Lizzie. I lit up a cigarette to show I was not in a hurry or desperate to fuck her on the beach or anything. We both had a smoke, and then we started kissing. She ended up on her back with me on top of her; I whipped out my cock instantly. It was ready and hard. I thrust it into her wet pussy. Three or four thrusts in, I heard a couple of sounds like there were people around.

I looked up closer into the surrounding darkness and you would not believe what I could see. There were three random men hovering around the corner with their penises in their hand. Extremely terrible and shocking. I could not believe my eyes. Lizzie started crying. I was in so much shock that I started laughing. I stood up and the guys all sprinted off into the darkness. My girl was quite shaken, along with Hayley and Ed.

Basically, it was clear Lizzie wanted to continue having sex with me. At this point, it was about me making her feel safe. Making her know that she was ok with me and that I would look after her. A few kisses and cuddles helped re-affirm that. The walk back to their apartment took around ten minutes.

We got back and the four of us sat in the balcony for a little re-cap of what had just happened on the beach. The girls were now starting to see the funny side. And we made jokes like "what if he was Justin Bieber", would you let him join in? That sort of stuff.

We drank for a bit, and then the mood was becoming right again. Well, a little bit until Lizzie ran off to the bathroom to throw up. Was I going to fuck a girl who had just thrown up? Yes, I was, she brushed her teeth "with her own toothbrush" unlike my situation with Anna a few rows up from here.

After that, she jumped in the shower and asked me to come and shower her. It wasn't like a messy one as she had already been in the shower for five minutes. I jumped into the bathtub behind her, both of us under the shower and I fucked her from behind. This felt fucking incredible until Ed walked into the bathroom whilst I was cumming in her mouth after my second orgasm.

I then fucked Lizzie again in the bedroom, after a couple of hours, the remaining four of her friends came back, three of them with guys and one without. The one without a guy then went outside and actually started giving blow jobs to random dudes as she was so desperate to also get laid like her friends were.

This was a whole new world to me, the word of crazy 18/19-year-old girls who lose all principles on holiday. I had a great night with Lizzie though, she did get a bit attached to me over that week. I had to cut the strings as this was just holiday sex and nothing more.

We never kept in touch after the holiday, but we both would admit that we would have preferred to have completed our sex session on the beach without any disturbance. This was my only regret of the whole experience.

ROW 19

BOOBS FOR A LIFETIME

AUGUST 2012

It was still the summer highlighted by my time on the Spanish beaches. I had lived in big cities all my life and I fancied a bit of a change. Some sun, sand, sea and beach. Preferably some nice tits too. This was what I was about to get.

I had a job offer at a large financial organization in the coastal town of Bournemouth. So I relocated there for work from London. It was a nice town. Nice, friendly people and a very good lifestyle. I had found a place to live with a new colleague of mine who had a spare room. It was all becoming a good experience here.

I was out of London my city, my playground where I had been all my life. It was time for Rex Wood to spread some seeds. Some seeds had already been spread North in Ireland. It was time to take this down South.

The weeks went well in my new job. I did the whole going out clubbing thing at weekends. My friends were also my colleagues, so I couldn't fully unleash the Rex you had read about so far. It took a couple of months, I focused on my job and my career and tried to make a good impression. Even the girls I worked with were none other than friends. I was finding this hard to get used to at the beginning.

Remember my views on boy-girl friendship. Every girl I met was put through the question in my head "would you bang her?" It's inevitable if a woman is semi-attractive. Well for me then, even if she wasn't. If she was over 18 and was breathing, you could say she was an automatic candidate for a smash. This is how classless I was at this time. A desperate dog, desperate to smash anything that walked.

There was a lady who pushed a trolley around the office building. I am not sure exactly what she did. But I think worked in the kitchen and she handled lunch delivery to desks. She always smiled at me and seemed to flirt from a distance and even I could tell she was eye-fucking me on more than one occasion. Women are usually very good at doing this without the guy even noticing. I loved it.

Right now while writing this, I am listening to 'Humble' by Kendrick Lamar. At the time, I knew this lady wanted me so bad, and if anything it made me far from humble. In other words, I was cocky as fuck. A lot of girls do find this attractive to be honest. Even though majority would fail to admit it.

My next conquest went by the name of 'Melanie'. I found this out when I eventually said hi, and she wouldn't stop the conversation. We said hi and swapped numbers in the same conversation. She clearly wanted to turn the eye-fuck into a real fuck.

I find it hard to believe I have waited these many paragraphs of this row to mention her boobs. They were insane and off the scale. They were the 9th and 10th wonders of the world in my eyes. They were so massive, that I think she had to have custom made bras. Her body itself was petite, and she wasn't really fat. Her boobs were probably 50% of her body mass. If you were to have a BMI measure for boobs mass index. Hers would be way up there. No exaggeration. Anyway, forget the long game, we swapped numbers on Wednesday.

On Friday, she texted me and asked me to meet her for a drink. I played a bit hard to get. I went out for a drink with my colleagues and was getting pretty smashed. It got to about 10pm and then I messaged her, asking where she was. She told me and I jumped in a taxi instantly.

I met her at the bar she was at with her friends. She dragged me to the dance floor, and believe it or not, because of our height difference, my dick was literally grinding on her boobs. I had never really felt this sort of sensation before, and neither have most people as there are very few people on this earth with such incredible huge tits. It got so tense and I couldn't take it anymore.

I told her I was tired and her answer was just what I wanted to hear. She was like "do you want to go back to mine and have a spliff and chill?" This sent shivers down my spine and butterflies through my stomach and my dick. We all have stomach butterflies all the time, but dick butterflies trust me. This was a million times better. So, we got in a taxi back to her place.

When we arrived, she rolled up a spliff. We smoked it and chilled while watching TV. We were obviously hugging and kissing at this point, so there was no awkward moment.

All of a sudden Melanie asked "Rex can I suck your dick?" I was like "sure". Haha. Always have to play it cool. She sucked it for maybe ten minutes and then, it was the moment of truth. I grabbed my dick out of her mouth and put it.... wait for it.... yes it is what you are thinking. I put my dick in between her huge tits until it was nowhere to be seen.

I then fucked her tits until I came all over them. These boobs were miraculous and definitely one of a kind. It was the first time in my sexual life when I wasn't that interested in sexual intercourse.

Half hour later, we fucked in her bed, and my best memories of that were Melanie riding me and her boobs making loud flappy sounds and me cumming so much. I stayed at hers overnight.

In the morning she made me a nice breakfast, whilst she had my dick for breakfast and again I went for the Milk on the tits option. What a night, definitely up there with one of the breast experiences I ever had. Well, make it two. I didn't stay at my Bournemouth job for that long so I never got to hang out with Melanie again.

ROW 20

CLINICAL REX

OCTOBER 2012

I was rounding up a short stint in Bournemouth as I had got a job back in the City of London in finance. I was going to become a "Banker". In my head, things were taking shape. I was about to elevate my social status in my eyes. This was going to mean "more women" indirectly. Believe it or not, it did make a huge impact as you will find out. I had a few weeks off before starting work in London.

I took time to catch up with friends and spend time with my family. I spent one weekend with my close friend Dean in Reading where he lived at the time. I arrived in Reading on a Friday night in October. If you are familiar with the academic year, as I was then you know this was around fresher's week or freshman week as they say across the pond. So there were a lot of events, parties and nights out. I also had missed university life and I wanted a piece of the action.

I dropped my bags off at Dean's place. He introduced me to his flatmates and we all drank and played FIFA together on Friday night. We went out to a place called Q-Bar in the city centre and to be honest I did kiss a couple of girls, but that was about it. I didn't get laid that night.

I mean after all I was in Reading to visit my friend. Believe it or not every guy, mostly the single ones have this ulterior motive. I was in Reading to see Dean and also try and get laid. Facts are facts so let's not get it twisted.

On Saturday night I carried on with the same routine again, I put on my best outfit. I felt very fresh and with good energy and we also had a great build up. I felt good. We went to the union again. On this night I remember being drunk and actually not giving a shit about whether I got a girl or not. I was just having fun messing around with the guys on the dancefloor, doing funny dances and shit. Four of five jaeger-bombs later, things changed a bit. By the way, a jaeger-bomb is a mix of Jaeger-master and an energy drink like Red Bull.

So, a few jaeger-bombs later I noticed a blonde girl drifting towards me on the dancefloor. Rex was ready. I cut the games, I pulled her hair and asked her "where did you get your wig from?" It obviously wasn't a wig, but she had really nice bleached blonde hair. She loved my approach and obviously flirted back.

The club was ending at 3am and I approached her at about 2:45 am. The perfect time, as I got to it straight away and knowing I had 15 minutes there was no need to play games. It was literally talk for five, dance for five, close the deal for five. Clinical! Obviously, I wasn't thinking so tactically. But that's the best way I can summarize it for you. Luckily, Dean had also got with her friend. Perfect. Two on two. It couldn't be better.

There is nothing more annoying than a mismatch where. I don't mind mismatches where there is an extra guy. But when there is a girl extra. In most cases, that girl suddenly acquires a PhD in cock-blocking. I have seen some of the greatest skills in the history of cock-blocking. One in particular which ended up with a cock-blocker faking sickness and ending up in A & E. You shall find out more as you read on.

On this night it was Dean, me and two girls. My girl was called Daisy. We walked back to their apartment because I suggested ordering pizza. Boom! Yes, for a girl after a night out, pizza works like magic. I think my pizza to smash rate is about 90%.

So, we got back to their apartment. I ordered some domino's pizza. We all ate together, Dean and his girl went to her room. I was in Daisy's room eating the rest of the pizza. We ate till we were really full. Pizza worked like an aphrodisiac. The more the pizza digested, the more horny Daisy was acting. She slid my clothes off all of a sudden and gave me head. It wasn't the greatest head, however, I cut it short and just fucked her. We fucked once at night and once in the morning.

My Weekend had ended up being really good. I had a nice day on Friday with the guys playing FIFA and drinking. Messing around, a good night out on Saturday when I wasn't even focusing on attracting women for once. She walked right into me and she got laid.

Daisy and I messaged a couple of times after. For me, there wasn't really much attraction other than the initial attraction which led us to fuck each other. She seemed happy to keep it as that and so was I.

ROW 21

BREAKING TOO MANY HEARTS

FEBRUARY 2013

Remember my friend Dean, who was with me when I shagged Daisy. We went on this mini going out spree afterwards. I had stumbled on a club in South West London in a place called Putney. This was to be the venue for several of my nights out over the next couple of months. I had met up with Dean and we headed over to a Wetherspoons pub across the road from the club.

'Wetherspoons' is the name of a brand of a chain of pubs all over the UK. They usually are very well priced and are very friendly if you are counting your pennies whilst still requiring a decent quality of food and drink. We started off with a £6 bottle of red wine each. This was literally all we needed to get us to feel great and in the mood for a great night out. Mix that with one or two jaeger-bombs and we were flying.

We headed over to Fez club at about 11:30 pm on Saturday. The crowd was sort of like a typical west London club and full fairly well-educated young people. I was the king of this. I was so good at seducing girls of this kind having honed most of my game by smashing girls from my university.

One thing I had not really done at this point was extending my geographical range of the girl's origin or nationality at this stage of the spreadsheet. I was in the best place in the world to do that though.

I was not really one to have a type. As a guy, some days I feel like sleeping with a blonde girl, some days I feel like a brunette, some days a Rihanna-lookalike, some days something else. It just always varied with me. I guess I was just always attracted to beauty and sexiness. Beauty and sexiness cannot be nailed down to one look, shape or size as you will tell from the varied looks, shapes, and sizes of the women on this spreadsheet.

We had been in the Fez nightclub for a few hours and it was the last hour of the night. We spent the night talking and flirting with several girls, mainly in the smoking area. The smoking area was in a weird place. It was behind the club and you had to walk two flights of stairs. It was very cosy and gave you the opportunity to chat to and scope out people you had seen on the busy dancefloor.

This night, however, my conquest, or should I say, the lady who's conquest I became actually met me on the dancefloor. I had noticed her earlier but I didn't think that much of her as I felt like I had so much choice on the dancefloor.

As the club emptied, I then noticed a girl who I thought was a great dancer, I had never seen someone move so well on the dancefloor. I was literally seduced by her movement. I went over to her and jumped the gun by grinding on her. I am not a bad mover myself, so we had a very nice dance on the night. Again, this was me doing the right thing at the perfect time.

I danced with her until the end, and my friend Dean danced with her friend. My girl was called Natasha. She was of Greek Origin but grew up in Australia. She had a very interesting background, and again she was another Nurse I was about to fuck.

It was just after 4am in the morning and the club had just shut. We walked over to the Greek kebab shop around the corner and grabbed some food. The four of us ate pretty quickly, it was as though we were all pretty horny and wanted to get back and get laid ASAP.

We then walked all along Upper Richmond Road to Natasha's place. Luckily for Dean and I both girls shared a house. When this happens it's always great, to get a girl back and your mate comes back with her friend. It's even better when you get to go back to the same place and you can just hi-five each other the following morning. I am sure girls do the same when they have had a good conquest. I would like to think I have been a good conquest for one or two girls in my life anyway.

We got back to the girl's house and Natasha dragged me straight up to her room. Dean and her friend stayed in the living room downstairs. I remember we fucked straight away and we were so loud that they heard us downstairs and could probably describe everything we were doing from start to finish from the sounds alone.

We then went back downstairs and had a drink with Dean and her housemate. After this drink, it was back to bed for all. More and more sex. I remember being exhausted in the morning and being made a full English breakfast by the girls. This was the full monty, it was a dance in the club followed by a kiss followed by a kebab shop then home then sex before bed and then breakfast. The perfect night. I left her place a very happy man.

I did fuck her a few more times after that, but then we fell out when I got bored and cancelled meeting her a few times. She ended up getting pregnant with someone else's baby a few months after that. And yes it was definitely someone else's baby.

This was another Natasha and another bad ending; you could see why I was becoming statistical and superstitious about the name thing. I did miss Natasha's bum though pretty much a few days later. I think that kind of led me to the next girl you will find out about.

ROW 22

WHY DO I KEEP LEADING THEM ON?

MARCH 2013

A few weeks after my last encounter with Natasha. I met up with her for a drink and she just showed me hate. She wanted us to be together, but I had no interest in that. With her, it was 100% lust. At least I knew what I wanted and I think it's better to have said it then than go with the flow and hurt her even deeper later on. I decided to just carry on with my life.

Before I had ended things with Tasha, another night at Fez with Dean came up. We had the same club routine here as I explained from the night I met her.

On this other night, there were a lot of girls. There was one particular group which stood out -a group which had a blonde girl wearing a blue dress with a very nice bum. I could not stop looking at her all night. I eventually got the courage to go and speak to her. Her name was Sian and she worked in Marketing. We got along very well.

The group was a group of 3 again. Dean latched on to Heather, her friend. Unlike our past experiences with cock-blocking friends, the third girl Emily was very welcoming. It might have something to do with the fact that she was the prettiest. Strange one right? I went for the middle ranking and Dean went for the third one. I will explain my logic here. I went for Sian purely for her body. Remember I am Rex Wood, the boy who got on a 5-hour coach journey after a girl sent him a picture of her ass. If there was a good enough ass on the moon I would become an Astronaut and fly there. I just love a nice butt. They make me very happy.

So you know why I went for her now. As for Dean, I wouldn't say he was lacking in self-confidence or anything. It was more a security thing. He didn't want to take too much of a risk and go for the hottest one as she was more likely to be "harder to get", and so he played safe and went for the third best.

So, for you hot girls, when you find out that you might not be getting hit on as much as you would expect or are used to, perhaps give it a thought. Maybe the guy thinks he has no chance with you.

Remember, as a guy when there is one large group of girls, we have to be careful. We have to size them up. Have a preference, size that option up without making it too obvious. See if she might throw back the same feelings and then go in for the kill on the one you choose. After learning the hard way several times, this has been my approach. I spoke to Sian, and she was a bit shy, so for some reason I echoed her vibe. I played the nice, reserved, patient gentleman who was not interested in anything other than a chat.

We had a nice relaxed chat in the smoking area, then we went back downstairs for a round of drinks and some shots of tequila. The girls seemed to like us and invited Dean and I back to Sian's place. So let's do a count, it was two guys and three girls who went back. Sian and I slept on the sofa. Her friend Emily slept in her bed and Dean and Heather slept on the floor in the living room with us.

There was to be no action on this occasion. I woke up spooning Sian with the hardest dick known to man. Morning glory at its finest. I was definitely going to try and tap that another time.

I never get too disappointed if I don't sleep with a girl on the first night. I mean let's put it into perspective. I had met her in the last 12 hours and then we spend the night together. That means at some point I will eventually fuck her with the right approach. I went home and carried on with my life. We had obviously swapped numbers. The fact that I didn't even try to have sex with her the whole night was a bonus. To me, it was a sacrifice, an investment. After all, I still got to spoon her amazing ass all night.

I kept the texting game going. I wanted to keep the momentum going as I obviously had a goal of bedding Sian. I won't lie, it then turns into a challenge. In most guy's minds, when it turns into a challenge then that's it. I was then focused on pretending I wasn't that interested in sleeping with her when that's all I was interested in. Everything I did and every game I played was towards sleeping with her.

This opens up another debate. From a girl's point of view, is it better to make a guy wait before having sex or do you get it out of the way early and then focus on other things. I am definitely a fan of the latter. The reason being that if you were to hold out, my focus 24/7 would be 'how and when I am going to fuck you'. Honestly. Whereas if we fuck early enough, we can then focus on other stuff and the other real things in a relationship. I think that approach is more logical.

Historically I generally ditched girls if I hadn't slept with them by the 3rd date. Who knows, my spreadsheet might have been longer. But on the other hand maybe not, maybe I might have been settled down and married. This is the butterfly effect we have to deal with.

My texting skills were very good. I am able to keep girls interested for years and years even if I don't see them. On a given day, you might pick up my phone and you would see a 'hi' from a girl I shagged five years ago. It's all about leaving an effect on a girl. I had met Sian just the once, I had clearly left an effect on her.

"Who is this guy who didn't even try to sleep with me?" It came across as mysterious. She loved it. We met up the following week for a burrito and a cocktail.

My favourite first date combination. It was cheap enough for a first date whilst still being nice and classy. Well, I say "classy", but it's also funny to see how different girls eat their burritos. The awkward biting and looking around, the messiness and self-consciousness. It's interesting to see they all act in that situation.

I used to take girls to the same burrito place on first dates. I took about twenty-five girls there including Sian. The waiters there just giggled and you could see the look of "Oh it's Rex again". I was so comfortable here. It became like my home turf and I was successful with about 90% of the girls I brought here. So when I mention a first date in the book moving forward, you know that we most likely went for a burrito and a cocktail.

Sian impressed me by grabbing the burrito and going in full on. It was a good date. We also had a few drinks afterwards. But oh dear me, afterwards she hugged and kissed me and said "bye I will see you soon". "Is this bitch crazy?" I thought to myself. Obviously, I was pretty composed and I smiled and said "yes definitely". This was turning into "dating each other". It wasn't how I ever saw it or what I wanted with her.

Remember it just started off with the way her ass looked in the blue dress. But I never felt like "yes I could date this girl". I was enjoying hanging out. I wanted to sleep with her and see how it felt. We obviously had completely different ideas of what we wanted with each other.

On the second date, I kind of had no expectations anymore at this point. The one positive was that we chose a place close to hers to go for dinner. This then got me feeling pretty optimistic. We went for dinner and a drink. We both had burgers, she ate that better than the burrito for sure.

Afterwards, we walked back to hers after stopping over to get wine from the supermarket. A few glasses of wine later, we started kissing and then the moment you have all been waiting for. It finally came. Reverse cowgirl on the couch we had first slept on together two weeks earlier. Boom! Rex was in there. I proceeded to fuck her in every part of her flat. I remember the sex was so loud that I felt like I needed earplugs. This was most definitely triggered by the long wait and build up. A great session. I spent the night at hers and we had sex several times that night.

I saw Sian about three more times and then I got bored as I only wanted to have sex with her. I got put off by the fact that she started planning things to do together.

Just to let you know, there was an overlap and yes I was sleeping with both Natasha and Sian at the same time. I preferred Sian, hence I ditched Natasha and was happy to keep smashing Sian. I was seeing her for months and then she started asking commitment questions like "what are we"? "Why don't you want to commit to me". She started planning six, seven months in advance.

I think I am a pussy sometimes. Or well I was in the past. I would keep leading a girl on until I found a substitute or one better.

I led Sian on for months. I did love hanging out and I enjoyed her company. We saw each other for around two months. Believe me, it was two months of good sex and I have no idea how it even ended.

ROW 23

STUCK IN MADRID

MAY 2013

I had ignored Sian for weeks as I felt she was getting too intense after. In the early hours of one May morning, I had been on a night out. I didn't pull, there was no "last chance Lucy". I went to the chicken shop after the club. Still nothing. I was horny.

Driven by my hormones, I went straight to Sian's place like a psycho at about 4am. I called when I was on my way. She was obviously asleep and picked up and said "are you okay?" I told her I missed her and asked if I could come over. She sounded excited. She obviously did like me and would have liked to actually try and possibly build something together. I hated myself for doing that but like I explained earlier, I wasn't thinking with the brain in my head.

I got to her place and she let me in whilst still half asleep. We got into her room and we got straight to business. Straight to the sex that I came for. On this particular night, I just fucked her doggy style against the chest of drawers. The sex was sensational as I had been a bit horny that evening and fired blanks in the club.

These are the moments when hard work pays off. You have this portfolio of girls who you can always call on at any time of the day and they would always be there for you. It's tough though because eventually they always want something in return.

This turned out to be the very last day I ever saw Sian. I slept for a couple of hours and then we woke up and she drove me home. I didn't even message her again. That was cruel I thought. But I just felt uncomfortable by how emotionally close she was getting.

I was getting more ruthless and finding it easier to dump girls. This was obviously helped by a Bank holiday weekend trip I had planned with two friends Angelo and Richard. We were headed over to the beautiful sunny city of Madrid.

We flew over on the Friday of the long weekend. We landed in Madrid and got a taxi to our Hostel. Yes, hostel. I was a bit of a spoilt kid who had never stayed in a hostel. I rowed with both friends in the taxi when we arrived. I wasn't too impressed by the place we were staying. How the fuck was I going to bring girls back here?

I eventually got over where we were staying and I was having a great time in Madrid. I was really liking the city. I was meeting girls everywhere. On Sunday night, Angelo and I went to a club called "Joy". It was very merry in here. A great atmosphere. We had good laugh and banter and met some cool Brazilian transsexuals who we had a round of tequila shots with.

We were really enjoying Madrid. We went to the dancefloor. I assumed my position. Right on the edge where I could get a good view of most girls. One caught my eye. A brunette girl with a great smile. Rex went into lion mode.

I went over and spoke to her. Her name was Roxanne and she was from Seattle. Whoops, I was in Madrid and I found the American again. Rex and Roxanne, we definitely sounded like an amazing couple. I remember we had the usual "where are you from?" conversation. She was on a two-week Euro-trip with a friend. It was like perfect.

We danced for a bit. I made her laugh a couple of times. We kissed and messed about. I declared my interest in her by being all touchy. Hands on her waist etc. She loved it. She was feeling me up too. My arms, my back, my butt everything. Lust was in the air in Madrid. She was clear and straight to the point. She wanted to fuck me. She found it a massive turn on the way I confidently approached her in a club full of guys being so perverted and not knowing the right way to approach a girl.

The best and the worst parts of this night were yet to come.

We left the club together, I left Angelo in there but I let him know when I was leaving. I didn't believe my eyes what was about to happen. Roxanne was crazy, and I fucking loved "crazy". We walked out of "Joy", but I was about to have my own "joy".

We walked maybe for one minute and there was a hotel on our path. This girl went in there and asked for a room. She paid for the room and dragged me up in there. We took off our clothes as fast as we could and we just fucked each other for about two hours. Bearing in mind this was supposed to be my last night in Madrid, as I had an 8am flight back to London.

I woke up at 6am ready to leave, and then she started sucking my dick again. Let's cut this long story short. I missed my flight back home. But you know what it was very worth it as I spent the whole day having passionate sex with Roxanne.

ROW 24

BEST OF A BAD SITUATION

MAY 2013

I was stuck in Madrid. My friends had got on their flight back home. I had traded my flight ticket for a day in bed with Roxanne. In my opinion, it paid off often if you have such spontaneous sex. We went from dancefloor to sex in probably under two hours. The fact that she found the nearest hotel and got a room there on the spot made it even more special.

It got to about 4pm in the afternoon and Roxanne had to leave as she was continuing her journey through Spain with her friend. I had decided that since I had missed my flights I would stay a couple more nights in Madrid. I was loving the city so why not?

I checked into a proper Hotel. I called in sick at work and I was happy to do that for another day or two. My friend Angelo had contacted a girl who we became friends with at the hostel. A Canadian by the name of Amanda. She felt sorry for me hearing that I was stuck and alone in Madrid. I was the only one in my life who wasn't feeling sorry for myself. I was loving Madrid and loved the fact I was there for another couple of nights.

I received a call from Amanda and she asked me to come over to the hostel. Yes, the same hostel from the beginning where I had stayed previously. I got there in time for the evening Paella and drinks. After which the plan was to have a pub crawl in and around the city centre of Madrid.

It was a round-table type set up. There were some new faces that had just arrived on the day. As always, one in particular caught my eye. As this was a chatty setup, people sat around the table talking. My best strategy was to talk and be active to other people, and to totally ignore the girl I was interested in. One of the best tricks in the book which works all the time.

I stayed true to my tactic with extremely accurate execution. I made no eye contact with her. I was laughing and making jokes with the other guys on the table. As the evening progressed, I could see from the corner of her eyes she kept trying to make eye contact and trigger an introduction. It was like "who the hell is this guy who just arrived and is giving me no attention?" "I'm bloody not used to that, I wonder what he is about". That's the vibe I got as every time I spoke to the group, she always turned to look at me and tried to make eye contact.

I eventually forced myself to smile at her while I was speaking. I could kind of tell that my smile melted her heart. As I had become good friends with Amanda, I was able to use her to make the other girl jealous. She longed for my attention.

I found out she was called Isabelle after Amanda eventually introduced us. She did it in the best possible way by explaining why I was stuck in Madrid but without going into too much detail. Yes, the words mysteriously and curiosity came to mind.

Things were going perfectly. It was as if I had read "Sexcellence - The Sex Spreadsheet". I came across as mysterious plus not giving her any attention. She became curious, and then partially found out that I was in Madrid through crazy circumstances.

By the time we headed off for the pub crawl, she had isolated me from the rest of the group and we got talking. She explained she was visiting Europe from Canada where she was from. She was travelling as a two-some with her mate from home.

You see this whole thing wasn't all easy for me. There were other guys there. I remember identifying two other guys who were making their moves. It was a jungle. I had to keep my feet grounded and stick to the basics. The basics I knew had served me very well all my life. Each of the other guys had their fair share of a chance with Isabelle. I think there was a point where I wasn't even near her for close to an hour.

In the time I kept myself distracted with the other guys and girls present. I made sure that when we got in close proximity I didn't stay around for too long. I also made sure that I kept the eye contact going. More like responding to her stare with a smile as opposed to constantly staring at her.

Eventually, she cornered me and tied me down. I think she had had enough of my perfection at the chasing game. She nailed me down. We then got into a nice conversation, and she was telling me about herself and how she had just broken up from a long-distance relationship with a guy and she didn't want to have that anymore etc. I was like "errr...". I am not sure what she was insinuating there. But anyway I literally told her to "shut up" and I just kissed her. The surprise factor. She then grabbed me, and not only that. She asked where I was staying.

We went back to mine and had a smoke on the balcony. She started her chat again. I listened for a bit and then we got intimate which led to another night of sex for me in Madrid. That flight was definitely worth missing. She did not want to stay the night so I walked her back to her hostel at 6am feeling like such a proud man. The execution was perfect. I was becoming really good at this.

ROW 25

FROM THE DANCEFLOOR TO THE BED

MAY 2013

I had tried to reach out to Isabelle on my last day in Madrid. However, she was having none of it. It turned out there was a guy she had been seeing back in her home country. She felt guilty again. To her what we did was purely a one-night stand on holiday.

She did send a heart-warming message wishing me all the best in my future endeavours. She then blocked me on Facebook and on WhatsApp. If I needed conviction about that being a one-night stand that was it right there. This girl was really beautiful. It was hard for me to take in. I knew we lived in different countries and stuff. But to go from such a high from playing the game and having her in my bed and her blocking me everywhere a few hours after that did hurt.

I landed back in London a sad man. I was caught up. I may have been 27 years old Rex Wood "The Player" or whatever you would have called me at the time. But I tell you I was pretty hurt. I got back home on a Wednesday with a nice tan and glow from the Madrid sun.

My friend Richard asked if I wanted to go out on Thursday to a nightclub in central London called 'Jalouse'. The same actual venue is now home to a club called 'Tape'. Jalouse always had a good crowd and atmosphere. My favourite part of the venue was the chandelier's dropping from the ceiling as part of a special effect when certain songs were playing. This was really cool.

On this particular evening, I was feeling very confident. Richard and I chatted to a couple of groups of girls. We had some nice friendly conversations. We spent time between the smoking area and the dancefloor.

In the smoking area, we got chatting to two Swedish models. This is what I call "building it up". It works by starting off your night and just having casual conversations with anyone. Build up your conversation flow. Get in the mood. Without conversation skills, you would struggle to get with someone on a night out. It goes both ways. I would be put off by a girl who isn't able to engage me in conversation. No matter how hot she is.

We all subconsciously rate people the first time we set eyes on them. That rating fluctuates the longer you see them for. You might see them on a darker side of the club and then you might see them at the bar where it's brighter. Then you think slightly better or worse of them. The moment you speak to them however that's where the real impression is made. So on this night, I spoke to maybe four of five girls just for the sake of it and with no intentions. You could say I was laying seeds for the rest of the night.

From a guy's point of view, I would suggest if you are going to speak to several girls on a night out, try and make the conversations casual. Don't hit on every girl. Scratch the surface of each one if you prefer to talk to several. It does multiple things for you like build your confidence and gets you in the right conversation flow ready for when you find "her".

The "Jalouse" chandeliers came down and lit up the dancefloor. The good thing about this was I can imagine any girls who had seen me got to see me better in the light. The next thing I know there was a group of three girls dancing in front of us. One was dancing in a way I could not avoid looking at her. She then crept up and started backing up on me. I grabbed her by the waist and danced along. This was to be the longest single dance of my life. I ended up with my back against a pillar with her grinding up, down, left and right on me. I was loving this.

At one point her skirt got lifted up so high that I was dancing with her bare ass. She even turned around every now and then and rubbed my dick with her hands. This was either going to be a massive tease or a girl who knew what she wanted and was actively being direct and going for it.

I am never presumptuous in this situation. I had previously had experiences when girls undid my trousers and got my dick out on the dancefloor. Both situations never led to anything more. So at this point, I just tried to make conversation with the girl and see what she was about. Her name was Catherine and she was another Irish nurse.

It seemed I attracted the same type of girl time and time again at several times in my life. There's even another Irish nurse I met once who did not make it to the spreadsheet because we didn't have a condom. We ended up rubbing each other's private parts until we both came.

I spoke to Catherine and we went to the bar and got a drink. I met her friends and things were going well. It is very important to please a girl's friends especially when they are in the most powerful position to ever cock-block you. At this point, they are like the "Queen" on the chessboard who is trying to protect the "King". You have to handle them with care.

I was nice, calm and patient with her friends even though in my mind Catherine had turned me on so much that I just wanted to go back and have sex with her.

Eventually, the club ended and it was still about patience. I had to go to the cloakroom with her and her friends. They also lost another friend, and we had to wait till they found her. My thought process was manic. I also had to be work at 9am in the morning, and it was after 3am at this point. I soldiered on patiently, after all I was too far in to give up.

We eventually all got into a taxi. Yes, Catherine and I and her three friends. We had to drop them off at their different houses and at about 4:15 am we arrived at her place.

I then had to sit in the kitchen and endure a drunk conversation between her and her flatmate. I literally had enough and I asked where I could sleep as I had work in the morning. This triggered her sex instincts. It was as if she thought she had me but then I acted as though all I wanted was a place to rest my head.

She immediately ushered me into her bedroom. It was now about 5am. The memory is blurry to me now but we had very passionate sex. It's like we both went through such a long build-up with several obstacles in the way from the dancefloor to the bed.

ROW 26

CELEBRATING WINGMEN AND WINGWOMEN

JUNE 2013

I was tired after the first night with Catherine. The price for great sex was lack of sleep and a horrible day at work the next day. Luckily though it was a Friday. I had a trip arranged to Newcastle, a place which has quite a bit of history for me. Well not so much history at this point on the spreadsheet, but you will find out the type of history by the end of the book.
Newcastle was a great trip.

On the trip, there were a bunch of guys, some of my good friends who are mostly on the spreadsheet as wingmen. I love to give credit to wing-men and wingwomen. Without them, I would probably not have slept with half the number of people I have. I am confident and good enough to talk to a girl on my own. But it helps so much knowing you have that person around and you don't look like a lonely weirdo.

On this Newcastle trip, I had Angelo, Brad, Chris, Kyle, Kenny, Neil, and Paddy. If you know Newcastle, then you know it's a great city to party. We had two nights there on this weekend. We arrived on Friday and headed to a club called "Tup-Tup".

Here, I did meet quite a few girls but I was in no mood after the night I had with Catherine. I was tired and needed my bed. So out of selflessness, I decided I was going to be a wingman for the night.

I became everyone's wingman. I was talking to girls I didn't even like, just so that they could have their time with the girl's friend who they liked. It was fun because I had nothing to lose. I think I ended up kissing a few girls I was not even into. I am proud to say that on this weekend, four of my friends got laid.

I do love being a good wingman. I like the fact that the pressure is off me. The worst part of being a wingman is the part of having to talk to a girl who might be far from "your type" so to say. Or someone you would not even consider in a "last chance Lucy" situation. My happiness playing this role that weekend might have been due to being smitten with Catherine. She was hot and I wanted to see her again.

I definitely get my fair share of good wingmen and wingwomen. If you recall Amanda from the "stuck in Madrid" row, without her I would not have bedded Isabelle.

My fortune with good wingmen was to continue a couple of weekends after the Newcastle trip. It was a Friday night and I had planned to go to "The Roof Gardens", a nightclub in Kensington, West London. My friend Richard was coming round to my place and we were going to have a nice "pre" so we could head out feeling good as it was quite pricey at the club. Before coming, he asked me if he could bring his friend along. I said "okay that's fine".

Richard turned up with a young lady by the name of Suzanna. She was a petite Armenian. Very cute and almost Kardashian-Esque in appearance. I am sure you are thinking "poor Rex... how could he deal with all these females coming into his life". I was now also fully seeing Catherine around once a week and we were having very good sex. I was a happy man.

Now my friend brings a hot girl to my house to drink and go out with us. He said to me that they were 100% friends and that I could go for it. Wow, you could not wrap this up better Christmas gift wrap. I literally rubbed my hands together feeling confident and said to myself. "I am going to smash her". We all had a few glasses of wine and then had a nice little build up to the night out. We headed to the club. I had some amazing experiences as The Roof Gardens and so it became my regular spot of choice.

I did not really hit on Suzanna for a while. I waited to see what was out there in the club and to see if I could create a pool of options for myself. So we got to the club and everything was still casual. The club had an amazing outdoor area and the weather was good so everyone was outside. This made it easy to get involved with random conversations very easily. I did get chatting to a few girls as Rex does. The night went on at the same pace.

I left Richard with Suzanna for a while and then I spoke to a few girls here and there. I even went to the bar with another girl. I was having a good time.

About 45 minutes later, Suzanna and Richard came to look for me outside. This was the moment. I could tell she was starting to show interest after seeing how charismatic I was whilst around other girls. She saw me receive attention from other girls and me not giving a shit about the attention. I showed off a mentality of "yes... this happens every day". Even though it definitely didn't.

Why is it that girls give you more attention when you are out with another girl? I would need someone would need to explain that to me one day. Well, I was definitely using this all to my advantage. It was a vicious cycle. I was out with a girl who I looked nothing but friendly with. Her presence then helped me get attention from other girls. This then triggered jealous emotions from the girl I was out with. It was a perfect set up.

All along my friend Richard found this amusing. I said to him "look what you have caused". He was like "I think Suzanna wants to smash you". I laughed confidently but trying to be humble and keeping my feet on the ground. I did not want to be complacent with this as I had been in situations where I threw away opportunities because I thought they wanted me so much and I got cocky and lost focus instead of sticking to the same principles.

I was not going to mess this one up. I then looked at Suzanna, in her amazing white dress and nice shoes. I thought to myself "I am going to fuck you tonight".
At this point, the right ingredients were there.

Everything was laid out on the table for me. I just had to put it all together and prepare the dish. She was a beautiful girl, very hot. Amazing long dark hair, very nice dress and very nice shoes. There was no doubt she was interested in me. I was clearly interested in her. I had seen her show jealousy towards other girls. Richard who was her close friend told me he could tell she wanted to fuck me. If I fucked this up with all this evidence and proof then I would have just retired and closed and sent the spreadsheet to the recycle bin.

Instead, however, I wasn't going to let this happen. I went in as Rex does. There was a moment I dragged her to the dancefloor and then we went to the bar for a drink and then I just kissed her. I have never seen a woman's hands come alive so much. The kiss gave her the green light to literally physically assault me with her hands. It was as if she had more than two hands. Her hands were like on my dick, chest, bum, back, arms, and shoulders at the same time. I don't know how she did that. I was wearing a white shirt and I didn't check, but I am sure it would have had her fingerprints all over it.

What I did here with Suzanna I made her so hungry for it, and it was clearly building up. She wanted me and she made it clear. But she only went for it after I made the move with the kiss.

As guys, sometimes girls make it obvious. We then need to make the move, but we need to be clever about the timing and the approach. What we should never do is let a girl's interest distort our plans or the way we behave. In this example, I came out with Suzanna and Richard. I could have just stayed with her all night, if I did I probably would have gone nowhere. Instead, I engaged other females. This ended up being the catalyst which I needed to get with Suzanna.

After all the touching, we then left the club without telling Richard. Well, I messaged him saying we left. We got on a couple of night buses and went to her place. It was a nice flat in Bermondsey in London. On the way, we got some food and we had a nice dinner date in her bedroom. We were both pretty drunk and had rough sex after eating. She made me tea and then jumped on me before the tea even cooled down.

In the morning, we had sex again along with a breakfast of bacon and toast. This was a nice girl who knew how to treat a man. She then gave me a back massage and I left her place a happy man that day. However, there was still a lot of stick to come from this later on.

I left Suzanna's place and I planned to keep in touch. She seemed to show guilt when I was leaving. Being an emotional person naturally myself and having been through a lot of heartbreak at school from girls I liked.

I evolved in a way where I am able to nullify disappointment from one girl by offsetting it with the positivity from another. I always managed girls like this.

Also having an obsessive personality meant I needed to protect myself by spreading affection amongst multiple girls. Meaning I would be obsessed with no one.

This then meant that I would not get hurt if any of them decided to hurt me one day. This is not a good way to be but if you want to understand why some people are hard to get close to, then this could be a feasible explanation. I was that sort of person.

I kind of thought I could see Suzanna again, but she felt like she was a slut for sleeping with me. She was also worried about what Richard would say to their group of friends. This meant she wanted nothing to do with me. I thought how could she wake me up with a massage and suddenly not want to see me again.

I called Richard and he just went on about how much of a slut she was. If she was a slut then what was I? In fact, I think it's very unfair to call women sluts when they do exactly the same as us. Well, you could say we are all sluts. We should scrap the double standards

ROW 27

THE BOAT PARTY MESS

SEPTEMBER 2013

I needed to meet up with Suzanna the following week as I had left my watch at her place. And no, I did not leave it there on purpose. We arranged to meet at a burrito restaurant near her place. I was thinking perhaps she had got over the guilt and that it could be like a date and we could speak and maybe potentially see each other again and again. But no, it was not going to happen.

I waited there for about ten minutes and she arrived. She was not looking very happy at all. She didn't want to see me. I think Richard had caused her a lot of embarrassment by saying she was a slut and embarrassed him by sleeping with his friend. It was that sort of situation. She didn't want to be anywhere near me. Fair enough, I was nice to her and I gave her a nice hug and a little Rex kiss on the cheek. That didn't even put a smile on her face. She then left and I had a burrito by myself.

I just laughed inside at the whole thing to be honest as it wasn't really my fault. But I just felt like there was no need for her to feel guilty for doing something she had a right to do. Well, that was it and she wasn't interested in seeing me again.

I got over it pretty quickly as I was going to Brighton on the South Coast of England with Catherine from Jalouse the following weekend. Yes, I was still sleeping with Catherine. We ended up having a good weekend in Brighton. We did keep in touch and were still seeing each other weekly. As mid-summer came though things slowed down as she was off to Barcelona for a couple of weeks and I also had a trip planned to Ibiza for a week.

Bring on Ibiza, the party capital of Europe. I flew there with my friend Angelo. It was just us two and we were pretty straight to the point with what we were there for. We were there for boat parties and clubs and women mainly. We weren't really into the drugs side of the island. We had about three-day boat parties booked, and of course, we were also planning to go out every night.

We stayed in the part of Ibiza called San Antonio. This was full of a younger crowd and was a bit further away from the main part of the town with the super clubs. We spent most of our days at the "Ocean Beach Club". It was a week full of a lot of drinking. Both daytime and nighttime. From the beach club to a boat party to a club. We were sleeping maybe four hours a day.

We made friends with one of the security guys at Ocean Beach, Fernando. He liked us as a pair, and he knew Angelo and I loved boat parties. He gave us a special invite to a party on a private boat one afternoon. He told us it would be full of girls. Obviously, from the sound of that, anyone would give it some consideration. I felt like maybe he was bluffing. But we decided to turn up anyway.

We arrived at the pier just before 4pm when the boat was meant to depart. I could not believe my eyes. It was like a dream. There were maybe 40 girls. There was the owner of the boat, Fernando, the security guys, the boat captain, the DJ and us. "Haha", I laughed to myself. It was like an "All you can eat buffet", and believe me we were pretty hungry.

The boat departed shortly after we all got on. The Ibiza sun was shining nicely. We were wearing swim shorts with all the girls in bikinis. Music was blaring. This was paradise. We sat in the corner as we knew we had the upper hand. We were not going to approach any of the girls. We had to be careful about this one. We knew the girls would see our every move. It was nice to sit and observe which of the girls would be brave enough to make a move on us.

Within a matter of minutes, there was a group of three girls, Amelia, Emma, and Lucy.
Amelia made the move and approached me, Angelo went for Emma. Remember what I said previously

about choice when there are multiple girls. His move made sense based on this.

I can tell you another reason why his move made sense. She was wearing bikini bottoms and was topless. Yes topless with only glued glitter covering her nipples. Try and picture that scenario. We were in heaven. There was a point when I was laying on the net of the boat with Amelia on one side and another girl on the other. The boat even parked up in a cave for 15 minutes and we could hear the music echoing. This was just incredible. You could not write the script.

The boat eventually docked after an hour and a half of incredible fun. The type of fun you never ever want to end. We docked feeling quite drunk. We then walked back to our apartment with the three girls we had spent most of the time with. I held on to Amelia and Angelo held on to Emma. And yes, she was still topless but the glitter remained intact. It was good glitter to be honest. I believe she had it stuck on there at one of the many professional glitter stores in Ibiza. I even had an animal glitter design made on my torso for a trip to a club called "The Zoo Project". It was gorgeous stuff.

We walked back to our place. It turned out that the girls were staying in a hotel next to our apartment. Things were about to take a very different turn. Amelia and Lucy went to their hotel to get changed. Bearing in mind I had already kissed Amelia on the boat and we had got close, we had a good conversation and were getting along well. I kissed her and said "see you in a bit".

The plan was for them to get dressed and come back. The twist started when Emma decided she didn't want to get changed and she would come back to our room to have a drink. She wanted to remain topless. I think she liked the attention she had from the glitter. She came up with us and I must say things went downhill.

We were having a drink in the apartment and I noticed they were getting close. I was going to leave the apartment and let them have some privacy. Emma then called me back and said "No stay, I can handle you both". Yes, this actually happened. I was thinking I had got with her friend and never even really showed interest in her. I thought to myself "I am on holiday and I was single, and I had only known Amelia for about an hour".

I went back into the apartment and Emma had sex with both Angelo and I. She seemed to have wanted to do that all day and she took the opportunity when it came. She was in control of both of us the whole time and literally dictated what she wanted us to do. It was a very different experience for me. To be honest, Angelo and I could not believe what had happened.

About an hour later we had a knock on the door. Emma was obviously quite loud. The knock on the door was from the now forgotten Amelia and Lucy. We took a few minutes and then we let them in. To then it was a sight of utter disgust. It was clear what had happened. We then witnessed a row between the friends. They started calling her names and insulting her etc. Angelo and I just had another drink and stayed out of it. What a mess. We only wanted to go to a boat party.

ROW 28

STARS AND STRIPES

NOVEMBER 2013

Angelo and I arrived back from a crazy week in Ibiza exhausted. It was very exciting and highlighted by the crazy threesome if you like. I never spoke to Amelia again. I did send her a text of apology for courtesy purposes. I believe they kicked Emma out of their hotel or something and she had to go somewhere else. Craziness. What a trip.

I took a few weeks of going out at this point. After these couple of weeks off, I had a night out with my friend Gary and we went to the Roof Gardens for a casual night out. We bumped into a girl we had met at University, Tessa. She was Gary's love interest and pretty much "the one that got away" from his point of view. She was out with a girl called Cat. Cat was pretty with very nice eyes. She came across as freaky. We got along very well and we hit the dancefloor to let Gary and Tessa sort themselves out after all the years of being without.

Tessa and Cat lived together, so we ended up going back to theirs after the club. Gary and Tessa were obviously going to have sex. I was pretty much there just to keep them all company and obviously to try it on with Cat. The most that happened for me was being silly and showing her my dick and her holding it. We got a bit close in the bathroom and teased each other with our hands. She didn't want to have sex with me that night. I accepted it and I said we should go on a date instead.

We met up the following Wednesday, I chose to meet at a bar in Covent Garden called "Verve". I believe it's now called "Scarlet". We met up there and as it was a happy hour we went hard on the cocktails. It was a great night and Cat was wearing an amazing dress.

All was going well but then she started being annoying. She was getting cocky with me, talking about all the guys she goes on dates with. How she still sleeps with her ex, how she was too good for me etc. We then went out to the smoking area. There were a few other people there including a group of Americans. One of the American girls asked me for a lighter and then we got chatting.

Before I go further I would like you to put this into context for a moment. I was out on a date with Cat, she was pissing me off a bit with her comments and we were out in the smoking area and another girl starts talking to us.

I took interest in this girl. Her name was Jen and she was from Florida. She was a very pretty blonde. As I was on a date, we couldn't have much of a conversation. She asked me about good places to go out in London, and I cleverly or sneakily asked for her number so I can text her a list of recommendations of places to go out at the weekend.

At this point, I had lost interest in Cat, my date, but it would have been rude to ditch her at this point. Also, there was still a chance of sleeping with her and I had already put some good work in. The night ended soon after and I got in a taxi back with her. I got off at my place and the taxi took her home.

Let us pause on Cat for a moment. Two days later, on Friday which was also the eve of my 28th birthday, I text Jen, the American about meeting up that night and going for a drink to ring in my birthday. We agreed I would pick them up from their hotel at ten. I quickly rang up my partner in crime Angelo to come with me as a wingman because Jen was bringing her friend Kelly.

The plan was to pick the girl's up and then drop my car home and get a taxi to "The Roof Gardens". Angelo was to meet us there. I picked them up and we headed to the club.

In the club, I did the introductions of the girls to Angelo and vice-versa. We had agreed that Jen was mine and that he would go for Kelly. It worked out perfectly and we were all getting on. Jen was clearly very horny as was I. She kept making comments saying she could feel my dick while we danced. She even whispered to Kelly at some point saying "Big dick on my back" while I was dancing behind her.

It was such a great night in the club, and once the clock struck midnight, it was my birthday. I got a nice birthday kiss and shots from both girls. When the club closed for the night, the girls wanted to party some more. We headed over to an off-license where we bought a bottle of whisky.

Angelo lived around the corner so all of us went to his flat. He shared a flat with two other girls who were asleep when we arrived. We all headed straight into his bedroom. Don't worry there wasn't to be any group action this time. We had one girl each and I'm sure we were both happy with that.

I sat on his bed next to Jen for about ten minutes. She took her shoes and tights off and then whispered to me in her amazing American accent saying "I want to fuck you". I immediately ushered her to the bathroom. We got in there, we both stripped naked, turned the lights off and had wild sex. We were so loud that Angelo's flatmates woke up and were yelling and shouting. Jen was wild like me and we both ignored them and carried on for at least half an hour. While this was going on Angelo was having sex with Kelly in his room. I don't know what it is but I have always had a great time with American girls. What a way to ring in my 28th birthday.

ROW 29

THE YOUNG DREAMER

NOVEMBER 2013

Jen left London the following day with Kelly to embark on a tour of Europe. We kept in touch on 'Viber' at the time and she messaged me about how much of a great time she had and how she would love to sleep with me again.

She even invited me over to Amsterdam the following weekend, but I had an important family event, so I could not make the trip. I definitely would have loved to see her again, and she is one of the people I met in life who I would have loved to have another moment or two with. All I was left with was memories of a great night, and a 28th birthday I will remember forever.

A few weeks later, I received a text from a girl who I met at a club earlier in the year. Her name was Helena, she was a 21-year-old, very ambitious and determined girl. I actually met her while she was out with her friend and I was out with Angelo.

Helena and I had been on about five dates previously until I gave up on her as she was not putting up for me. I tend to be impatient with girls. Normally, if I don't kiss a girl by the second date or sleep with her by the fourth (sometimes third), then I lose interest. I am sure most guys have their thresholds, but I tend not to be the patient type.

There's the saying "good things come to those who wait", but in this case, I don't believe it's right to wait that long. What if you went on 20 dates and then had sex and it turned out to be crap, you would have wasted all that time, money and energy on each other. I am more a fan of "I like you, you like me", if we decide to be together or to date each other, then it should be natural to sleep together. That is just my view, but I am sure there are pros and cons to both.

With Helena, so I received this text from her asking how I was. I was thinking "haha, now she probably wants it". After making me wait so long and me giving up on her, she seemed so keen this time, at one point we started arranging to meet up. She just dropped the bomb and said "Why don't you just come to mine tonight and stay for a couple of days?" This was music to my ears as it was results of work I had done about half a year before that.

I obliged and agreed to go over to hers after work. She lived on the outskirts of London in a pretty part of Surrey. I arrived at her place, and she looked even better than I remembered. I walked in and she had set up the table with two wine glasses. It was very romantic, we ordered a nice Chinese takeaway and had a lot of wine. We spent most of the time catching up.

Obviously, I knew at this point that Helena wanted to sleep with me, but I still wasn't assuming anything. Even though I was at her place and we were eating, drinking, kissing and being merry. The main reason for this was I had been at her place six months before after that fifth date and she kicked me out the moment I tried to sleep with her.

I was enjoying all this as, she became so different, she was more straight to the point. We drank more and more wine, and then she bent down took my trousers off and started giving me oral sex. This was great. We then stopped and she dragged me off to the bedroom where we had sex for ages all around the room in all of my favourite positions.

I spent the night there and went to work from there. I also stayed for another night and we repeated the same cycle again. The next time I came round the following week, she started asking to look at my phone to see if I was seeing someone else. Obviously every now and then I had a repeat smash.

A repeat smash could have been any girl I had slept with in the past who came back into my life for at least one night. There were girls I had met out, and it was about who I was trying to meet up with or sleep with. I also had just got on "Tinder" the dating app at the time and was using it passively.

I definitely would not let her see my phone. Obviously, we were not even together or anything, but she kept talking and acting like we were going to be together. And being Rex, I keep doing this. I have to admit again that I did mislead her to think I did want to be with her in order to sleep with her.

But then on the other hand, I also did not want to be with her, but obviously, I could not commit at this point.

So, there was obviously no reason to rule out not being with her, it made sense for me to give her the impression I wanted to be with her. I think that's very fair. This was generally the approach when girls were proving too difficult.

For me, it was a case of mirroring and adapting based on each situation. So I didn't let her see my phone. She started to get pissed off. We continued to sleep together, and as she worked for a large fashion cosmetics brand, she used to shower me with gifts. I did enjoy that part. She was truly a lovely girl. For a few months, I was getting brand new perfumes before their commercial release date. I loved this about her. A very special girl.

She was only 21 and started making all these plans for us. She wanted to book holidays, she set dates up for us to move in together in her diary. She wanted to meet each other's family and friends. She made this plan and was telling me about it. I told her to slow down and let's see how it goes. She then got upset that I wasn't as committed as her. From my point of view, she was overexcited and just a young dreamer.

ROW 30

THE CIA AGENT

NOVEMBER 2013

I was still sleeping with Helena, but I was beginning to have enough of her pressure and stress. The sex was good and she was very motherly which was great.

There were really no problems other than her wanting to settle with me. It's funny because I was 28 and she was 21. She definitely felt like I might have been the one. Some of my friends who met her thought I should actually give her a chance and commit to her. But I wasn't ready, I felt like there were still things I had not yet done and I knew if I committed at that point I would 100% cheat.

Fridays in Banking were about drinks after work, and I mean heavy drinking with shots and bottles flying around throughout all the Nightclubs in London. I went to Bodos Schloss in Kensington one Friday after work. This was also the place where Helena and I had been on our first date. It was an Austrian-themed ski bar with very good schnitzel. It started off as a restaurant in the evenings and then became a club at night.

This might have been one of the drunkest nights on the spreadsheet that I remember. I was working in Canary

Wharf at the time. Canary Wharf is a major financial district in the east of London. I had been drinking with my colleagues at pubs there after work. We then made our way across London to Bodos Schloss to continue the drunk night.

I remember being out in the smoking area and talking to a random group of people. It turned out that they went to my University. I didn't know them, but they welcomed me into the group. The group was actually just one guy with two girls. The massive green light from them was probably because the guy and one girl were a couple. Once again Rex was at the right place at the right time. I can give tips but I would never be able to teach you how to do that.

The name of the third wheel was Rachel, and she was American who was working in London. She was very nice to me. All three of them were nice. I was having a good time with my colleagues, but I would say my night got better meeting these guys. We were enjoying the simple things like doing funny dances on the dancefloor and trying to replicate each other's dance moves. It was a really good night.

I felt comfortable enough to go in for the kiss with Rachel, and I did and it was very nice. We said we would go for one more drink as it was nearly the end of the night. She took me to the bar and said she would surprise me. It was my favourite shot of cafe patron. Perfect. We had the shot and left the club together.

She lived far from the club. I think we got on three night buses. One from Kensington to Piccadilly Circus, another from there to Tottenham Court Road, and a third from there to her flat in North London.

This was strange for me as I had stopped getting buses years before that, since University. However, it was a nice fun experience to do that with her. I think it did expose me to so many risks though. Each change of buses was a risk. We had two changeovers. At any of those points, she could have told me to fuck off. So I tried not to be too intense. I didn't even kiss her on the whole journey.

On the other hand, I am sure she was happy to have me with her as she was alone and it was about 4am. We finally got to her place, and until today I have no idea how we got there from the bus stop. It felt like it was on a hidden road, in a hidden building via a hidden lift and on an unknown floor. All I know was that it was an incredible view of the London skyline.

I got into her bedroom and I needed a quick trip to the bathroom. She told me to walk silently and tip-toe and make no noise and not turn on any lights. I had to use the flashlight on my phone, no joke. This was all so weird. I had no idea what I had got myself into.

I got into bed next to her. I didn't even bother trying to have sex, I think I just kissed her good night. I woke up in the morning, luckily still safe in her bed. She was being all weird. She "skyped" her parents and was up and doing stuff pretty early. She then stopped and asked me the weirdest question. She said "what can I do to make you leave? If I had sex with you now would you leave"? I replied "Hell yeah".

I then started to finger her, and she went "Oh you are really good with your fingers". She took her top off and after Mel from Bournemouth, I have to say she has the second best pair of breasts I ever had. These ones were a surprise as I couldn't tell from when I saw her with her clothes on.

We had sex for around fifteen minutes, and then I finished and she kicked me out. She didn't want to exchange contact details, so she created a brand new email address on Gmail in front of me and said I should contact her on there. I have no idea who she was, but she clearly wanted to cover her tracks for some reason. Perhaps Rachel wasn't even her real name and she was an undercover agent of some sort. What an experience!

ROW 31

LA PRIMERA SENORITA

JANUARY 2014

Being a regular on the London nightclub scene, I had made friends with a lot of nightclub promoters. One of whom was a lady called Majo. Majo was a beautiful Spanish woman, who I got chatting to on several nights at different venues in the city. She had helped arrange and organize nights out for my colleagues and I.

One night, I was at a club in London, and Majo happened to be there. She had told me in the past that she had a friend who fancied me after seeing me tagged on her Facebook. On this particular night, her friend happened to be out with her and in the same venue as me. From her point of view, it was a no-brainer to set both of us up.

Her friend was called Gemma, and Majo introduced us. She was very pretty with nice eyes and a nice body. She was wearing a silk top on a silk skirt with nice Louboutin heels. She looked pretty. Things did not always go perfectly for me as you might think. There was one problem, one obstacle.

Gemma was out with another guy. I asked Majo about him, and she said that he was her crazy on-off boyfriend. Pff I don't want to get involved with shit like that. Trust me, I have been involved with a few love triangles, and people with relationship issues, and I just prefer to stay out of things like that if I had a choice.

But then I have testosterone. I am not able to control certain aspects of my testosterone-led side. If a girl has a boyfriend, and I don't know her boyfriend so there is no breach of man-code.

If she wants to be with me or have something with me, it means I am better or I am doing something that her boyfriend is not doing. It means I am more of a man in her eyes to her than her boyfriend is and I will take that.

If she is bored of her boyfriend, then he is not entertaining her enough and it means I might be more entertaining to her. No matter how you look at it, he is definitely not doing something right.

I have met so many women in my life and I can say that 99% of them have the ability to be fully loyal and can be dedicated to one person. Or maybe it was just the way I treated them, I kept them entertained, and challenged. I always stimulated them and kept them relaxed, while still being on their toes.

Nothing was going to happen with Gemma on this night, but I told Majo to give her my number. The following Saturday, I met up with Gemma for lunch at

"Cote Bistro" in Kensington. It was a nice casual lunch and we drank beers. I only had one beer as I was driving, she had a couple. We kissed as we left the restaurant.

We then went for a coffee and she suddenly started giving me a blow job in broad daylight. I enjoyed this so much that I even started driving around randomly. It got to a point and I couldn't take it anymore, so I just drove her back to mine.

With Gemma it was very simple; we got back to mine and had a glass of wine on my balcony. We then went back inside and played some music in the living room. She was Spanish and she liked to dance, so we danced. She danced in a very sexy way.

It got to the point of no return when I just went in and undid her sexy brown shorts, I kissed her bum and slid her thong off. I turned her against the wall and fucked her from behind.

I am not sure I have mentioned many quickies in this book, but this was definitely a quickie. A great quickie, or as they say in Spanish "Un gran rapidity". Haha… I like the way that sounds. I actually asked Gemma how to say that after we had it. That's how I remember the phrase. Gemma also turned out to be the first of a few Spanish girls on the spreadsheet.

I drove up for coffee and sex with her a few times, we were good with this arrangement. The part I wasn't good with though was that she was still seeing her ex-boyfriend and he was also beating her up. This was absolutely terrible and offensive to see.

She would call me crying sometimes and I had to call the police. As I had been to her place to drop her off a few times, I gave them enough details that they were able to arrest him at her place at some point.

Domestic violence is something I stand against very strongly. The stats for these are appalling. I remember whilst working for Amnesty International as an 18-year-old, I found out that it was something silly in the UK 1 in 4 women and 1 in 6 men experience domestic violence in their lifetime. These were terrible figures.

So for once I did get emotionally involved to try and help this girl out because of my beliefs and principles. She was always very appreciative of me afterwards, as he got a sentence and she was able to obtain a restraining order against him.

Gemma obviously tried to contact me quite regularly since. Even as recently as 2016, I got a message from her on social media. I even had birthday cards sent to me in the post from her to my old address.

I know I have broken several hearts, but it is very nice to be able to make such an impact in someone's life.

I have heard and read of so many cases where domestic violence ends up tragically. I would advise people to take action the moment early signs of that start appearing in a relationship. I actually intend to do some more to help victims in the future.

ROW 32

I HAD NO "TYPE"

FEBRUARY 2014

Until now I had been with all sorts of girls, rich, poor, daddy's girls, spoilt brats, "sluts", angels, wife-materials etc. Whatever you want to call them or whatever they would like to be known as. Even with all this experience I was gathering and gaining, I still had no-type. It was like I had the craving for a different type of girl on a different day

There were several different days when my taste was one or more or a combination of the following; blonde, brunette, skinny, curvy, tall or short. I just did not have a type.

I met 95% of my girl on nights out at clubs, so I always restricted based on what type of girls are present in a club at a certain time. On one night whilst out with my mate Kenny, we were chatting girls up and we both started talking to a cute blonde called Maddy. She was very nice and very well-spoken and we got into a good career conversation.

Maddy worked with special needs kids and we worked in Finance. So it was interesting talking about the differences in our jobs. She was fascinated by the fact that I had had jobs working for charity. Even though my charity jobs were paid, girls seem to really like the idea that I did that. I liked the fact that she was more into those than the fact I was in Finance. We spoke for a while on the terrace which was overlooking the Thames.

For some reason, our conversation turned to biting after she said I reminded her of one of her patients. I felt like she was now actively flirting with me. She was so good, I couldn't read her.

I went into the club with Kenny, we carried on with our night as normal. I didn't think too much of the chat with Maddy and Kenny and I were now having a good boys night out.

Alas! I bumped into her on the dancefloor. We then danced like we had talked about previously. I made my move when I felt confident enough and as usual, the kiss happened. Again Rex-Style, this happened not long before the club was closing. I think I was at my most prolific in the last half an hour of a night out because I usually would have surveyed the club, tested it out with different people. Remember when I spoke about scratching the surface in the "from the dance floor to the bed" row.
I usually do this on nights out.

So, I knew my best option at this point was to go for Maddy as we had built such amazing chemistry during our earlier chat. I stayed with her and her friend, Sarah who she was out with. Kenny had left just before the end. So it was just me and the two girls.

You wouldn't believe what happened next. So we got outside the club. I didn't really try to go back with her as I didn't want to be pushy. We had a 10-minute conversation and a 15-minute dance and one kiss. I was going to go with the flow. Obviously in my head I 1000% wanted to sleep with her.

We got outside and she paused and said "It was nice meeting you Rex, we are going to head home". I was like "it was nice meeting you too Maddy, Let's swap numbers". So we swapped numbers at this point pretty quickly, and she walked to the main road about 100m away to get her Uber.

I was now waiting outside the club to see if there were any other girls left who I could potentially talk to. There also might have been some who I had spoken to inside. With these, I could just have continued from where I had stopped as Maddy was no longer an option for that night.

Two minutes later, my phone rang. It was Maddy. She said "Rex, come up to the main road, we are waiting for you".

I was Rex Wood, one of the post prolific bachelors in London, but I got startled and I definitely could not believe my luck. I dropped my phone in shock and it literally smashed against the pavement. I was in shock and now I had no phone. I picked up the broken pieces and sprinted nearly as fast as Usain Bolt to the main road. This was on "The Strand" in London I believe.

Maddy was waiting for me in her Uber. She explained to me that she told her friend Sarah that she really fancied me. Sarah told her to get me to go over as I was really "hot". Don't believe these girls, I am not hot. I am an average looking Londoner. What might be hot though is my approach.

I don't believe looks have that much to do with getting girls. Maddy clearly wanted me because of my mannerism and the way I played it cool with her, whilst making the moves at the right time. Some of these are hard to teach, but on reading about most of the lines on the spreadsheet, you should be able to understand a bit more and have a better feel for it.

We got back to her place in North London and went straight to her bedroom. It was another night of good sex for me. The morning sex was even better. We were like a couple. There was a lot of affection shown between us. You would have thought she was going to be my Maddy Wood if you had seen how romantic we were.

ROW 33

NORTHERN LIGHTS IN THE BATHROOM

FEBRUARY 2014

I was fucking Maddy for weeks and months, we were going on regular dates. We were like a couple. She was only 23 though. I ended up meeting her sister and her brother. Her family knew about me. It seemed like I was at a stage in my life where I was becoming that "eligible bachelor" that every girl I met actually considered as a long-term partner. I am sure this meant I was clearly doing something right.

The problem on my part was that I never went out looking for love. I was just enjoying the fact I was getting so many girls. I enjoyed partying and going out. My life was work, fancy restaurants, fancy holidays and fancy clubs. As part of all those I was getting access to so many girls. The supply was increasing as I got older.

One of my favourite week venues was actually an Irish pub in Leicester Square called "O'Neill's". I loved it there mainly because there were usually a lot of tourist girls there. It was also a nice casual venue with live music on one of the floors.

I was out with a bunch of colleagues on a Thursday night. We had gone for dinner at Asia De Cuba on St.

Martin's Lane in Covent Garden in London. We had a nice dinner and then we made the five-minute walk to the bar. It was a good turnout actually. I was with five or six colleagues. We were drinking beers, whisky, vodka, and shots of tequila and cafe patron all night.

I was usually the first to strike anytime there was a group of girls around. The first to make a move and always the most efficient.

There was a group of Norwegian girls dancing next to us. They were all quite pretty. I might as well gone for any of them; however, I chose one with nice legs and went for her. It was pretty easy.

I didn't need to say much I just grabbed her to dance. She loved it. She was kissing me within five minutes. To be honest, in this case, they were probably excited tourists who let their guard down and wanted to have a good time. There was no need for games here.

For me, the job was done the moment I held her hand to dance. She wouldn't stop kissing me all night. As she was in a large group, I then encouraged my colleague Jez to talk to her friends. He ended up getting with one too. The Norwegians were in town, and they were up for a big party and a lot of fun.

At the end of the night, Sex, and I had got with two of the girls. Mine was called Maud. She was cute with blonde hair and very nice blue eyes. We had a little problem though. Both girls wanted to stay together and didn't want to be apart. Jez and I lived in different parts of London. So, we had to come up with a suitable practical solution at the time in our drunk state. The main priority now was for both of us to get laid.

As we still had our other colleague Karl with us. We all went over to his place. It was a studio in central London. We got in an Uber and about ten minutes later we arrived at Karl's place, a studio apartment has a bed and kitchen in the same room and a bathroom separately. What happened next was pretty interesting.

Remember what I did with Jen in the "Stars and Stripes" row? I was about to do exactly the same. I didn't waste any time when we got in and I took Maud straight into the bathroom. We had sex in the shower and on the toilet seat. We were in there for around half hour when Jez started knocking on the door. He was ready to fuck her friend in the bathroom too.

I fucked Maud one more time and we came out and let Jez and her friend have the bathroom to themselves. Remember all this was on a weeknight. We had an 8:30 am breakfast meeting the next day. All I remember next was waking up in Karl's bed with him and Jez on either side of me. The girls had obviously left in the earlier hours.

The next day was terrible. We had to go to work in the same clothes, but luckily we made it to the breakfast meeting and had showers afterwards. I also remember going to a mall to buy a new set of clothes. We were living that "Wolf of Wall Street" life we dreamed about as kids.

ROW 34

THE LAYOVER

MARCH 2014

Jez and I were back at O'Neill's a few weeks later. If you have noticed so far, I usually go to places where I have built good momentum. So if I go to a bar or a club and I get laid from there, then I keep going there until I experienced a dry patch and exhaust the place. After which I then start going somewhere else. I think that is a very good way to decide where to go out.

We were walking around like we owned the place, obviously in a respectful way. I mean we were full of confidence. We did our regular tour of all three floors of the venue. There was a live band playing on the middle floor, so we hung out here for a bit. A few bar trips to get a bit more drunk, and then we were good to go.

I remember having my buttons ripped by a drunk girl who grabbed me to dance. I was walking around the bar with a shirt with three buttons missing. This was definitely not a good start. But Rex always tries to make the best out of any bad situation.

I also had no underwear under my work trousers. I had played football after work in Canary Wharf and had not brought a change of boxers with me. I definitely wasn't feeling like my usual "well-dressed", "well-prepared" self.

I spotted a blonde girl in a blue dress which matched the colour of my shirt. I think I walked over to her and said something silly like, "Could I please borrow some material to fill the gap in my shirt?" She laughed and said "No keep your shirt like that I like the look of it". This was good banter. We introduced ourselves.

So, her name was Lindsay, and she was Canadian and in London for one night on a stop-over whilst heading back to Canada from Germany where she worked. She was out with her friend who was just Jez's type and so they got along. Were we about to have back-to-back smashes with two friends? Only time would tell.

I was flirting with Lindsay as expected. I then told her I had no boxers on. I said it would be cool if she took her underwear off too. I literally meant it as a joke as I always mess about. The next thing I knew, she went off to the bathroom of the bar and came back to me swinging her thong at me. She was now wearing just the blue dress. She then sat on me and asked me to feel her down there. She was soft, wet and nicely shaven.

At this point, what was the point staying out in the bar? The momentum was pointing towards one thing. Unlike the Norwegian girls, these two didn't mind staying apart on the night. Jez was doing a great job keeping her friend happy. So, I left the club with Lindsay.

We then headed over to her Air BnB near Queensway in Central London. I don't actually remember sleeping that night. I think I had just about an hour of sleep or so.

What a stopover! 16 hours in London and she got to sleep with Rex Wood. I did try to keep in touch with Lindsey, but then she told me she had turned lesbian a few months after. Her WhatsApp picture even had a wedding photo of her married to her new partner.

I have no idea what I did to her. Perhaps she felt her experience with me was the peak of all heterosexual experiences and it was time to explore other options. I have no idea. This was now the second girl on the spreadsheet after Anna from "The victimisation of Rex" Row to turn lesbian a few months after sleeping with her.

ROW 35

FROM BREAKFAST TO REX'S BED

MARCH 2014

I was off from work for a few days, and my friend Angelo came to visit. We wanted to spend the day discussing some business plans we had. See, I wasn't all about women and partying. I also spent my spare time trying to do other productive things. Angelo arrived early one morning and we headed out for breakfast. We went to a cafe near Paddington Station in London.

I had salmon and scrambled eggs and he ordered a full English breakfast. We were having a nice morning meal and a great start to the day. We had some good plans for the day; we were going to go into some more details and planning for a business idea we were working on back then.

We were seated at the corner of the cafe. Two girls walked in with bags and sat at the table next to us. It seemed they had just arrived in London. We carried on as normal. After eating breakfast, we had coffee. I heard the girls were not from here as they had American accents. I built up courage and spoke to them. I had to build up courage as this was like 10am. I had never approached or chatted up girls in cafes or restaurants, and never at that time of the morning either.

This was a completely new territory and I was challenging myself by trying to achieve the same type of success out of my comfort zone. I spoke to the girls. Their names were Brianna and Fiona. They were Americans who lived in Spain, Madrid to be precise. That was great for me as I had been to Madrid, so we had a lot to talk about. They had just arrived and were visiting London for about four days.

We waited for them to have their breakfast whilst still chatting. Somehow we spoke about football and PlayStation games. I then invited them to my place to play FIFA 2014. They loved the idea. Angelo and I couldn't believe what we had just done. We were having breakfast and we actually got girls from the breakfast cafe back to my place with incredible ease.

Genuinely and true to their word, the girls came and we played on the PlayStation. It was still quite early in the day so there was no drinking. We played 4-player matches with one boy and each girl on each team. We had so much fun.

The priority here was to make the girls feel comfortable with us and trust us. We definitely achieved that. They stayed at mine for a couple of hours and then they decided to go back to their hotel around the corner for a nap. We agreed to meet later on to get some dinner and go for a drink.

When the girls left, Angelo and I gave each other high-fives. Like that was actually amazing. If they never came back I still would have been satisfied as that was impressive enough to be honest.

We met the girls later in the day at about 8pm. They both looked really nice. A lot nicer than they did earlier when we met them. We went to Benito's Hat near Oxford Street in Central London. We had burritos and cocktails as this was now one of my favourite first date combinations as I have explained in previous rows.

We all got tipsy here and then we went to a bar for another drink. We gave the girls an option of what to do next. We said we could go out that night to a bar and maybe a club. The other option, which was my preference, was to go back to mine and play drinking games.

We all agreed on the latter, this was a massive win for us. We went over to the supermarket and got some beers and some vodka for the games. When we got back to mine, we all decided to play "I've Never" also known as "Never have I ever". A famous drinking game which helps people find out secrets about each other. The game involves the first player making a statement starting with "Never have I ever". Anyone who has ever done the stated action takes a drink. This then continues round and round until the end.

We started off with nice simple things like places we had been and visited. After a couple of hours, it turned to things like anal sex, sex in public and threesomes. That was definitely the fun part. It got to a point when we were now pretty smashed. I could tell Brianna was the dirtier one, so I grabbed her and literally asked if she wanted to go to bed. She jumped at that option and we went into my bedroom.

We didn't mess about at all and we had sex that night as well as the next morning. I bet the girls never knew what their day was going to be like. But the most important thing was that we all had fun and that became the highlight of their London trip.

ROW 36

STREET GAME

MARCH 2014

Lauren, Street Game

March 2014 had been a great month for me. I was feeling super confident now not only in clubs, but also at other public places. I made Lindsay take her underwear off in a club. Later in the month, I had the experience with Brianna. All these were now showing me that I could approach and get girls anywhere and gain their trust.

I had been for work drinks one night, and stayed out a bit late. I got hungry and decided to meet my friend Gary at the Grosvenor Casino in Leicester Square. He wanted to gamble and I wanted to get some food.

I had not had any food all day and had been out drinking, so I was absolutely starving. I had some chicken wings and a burger while watching my friend lose a lot of money at the roulette table. It was now about 3am. He got pissed off and went home.

I left the casino at the same time and walked across Leicester Square to try and get an "uber" home from Piccadilly Circus. As I crossed the road to where Dstrkt nightclub was, I noticed a group of two guys and two girls. The two guys were visiting from Scotland and were in London to watch a Champions League football game.

I randomly said hello to one of the girls, and she grabbed me and told me to come with them. Her name was Lauren. So there were now five of us, three guys and two girls.

I went with them to the kebab shop where they grabbed food. The other girl, Sarah, was Lauren's friend from Uni. Sarah had got with one of the guys, Liam, in Dstrkt nightclub. Liam was out with his friend James. So the five us in the group were now Liam, James, Sarah, Lauren and I. Liam was happy for me to be around them as it seemed Lauren wasn't into James that much.

So I was walking home and I found myself now adopted by a stranger as a wingman and a girl who wouldn't let go of me. I thought to myself. "My life is fucking crazy, but I love it".

After they got food, it was now time to head back. The guys had a two-bed suite at The Grosvenor Hotel in Victoria. We all jumped in a taxi and went there. When we got to the hotel, there were two bedrooms with two Queen beds each. Liam and Sarah went into one room. Obviously, the other room was for James. Lauren and I took the other bed in there.

We jumped into bed and literally started having sex while James was trying to sleep. He was getting pissed off and shouted "why don't you guys just fuck off". This was a bit unfair considering it was his room in a hotel he and Liam were paying for and there was I, Rex, a random stranger shagging a girl who had rejected him.

Out of respect I stopped the sex and dragged Lauren to the bathroom. I fucked her in there for about half an hour. We then went back to bed. I woke up the next day, fucked Lauren again and then left to go to work. What a night! I hope we all now feel convinced that we can approach people anywhere.
It also does seem so much more fulfilling that hiding behind the dating apps of nowadays like Tinder, Bumble, Inner Circle and Happn.

ROW 37

WATERFALLS

APRIL 2014

I tried to message Lauren to see if we could meet up again. She replied saying she doesn't normally do one-night stands and what happened was a one-off and wished me all the best in the future. I think she only wanted to get laid that once as her friend was getting with Liam and she saw me as a better option than James. I felt used. But I liked it because she was actually incredibly hot. She showed me her Instagram photos that night and she looked great there too. We had each other on social network for a while also but never kept in touch.

It was time to move on. I was getting girls in all different parts of London. A night out with my university course friends was coming up. We had arranged to have "pres" at Chris's place in West Hampstead. About ten of us met up there and we went to Electric Ballroom in Camden.

The club was a cool venue. It had two floors which both had different but good music. There was also a good number of bars inside, so it was easy to keep drinking and get pretty smashed whilst already out.

I was about to have perhaps the worst "last chance Lucy" experience of my life. There was a girl who had been following me up and down from floor to floor relentlessly. I didn't give her the time of the day. I just felt like I didn't fancy her at all the whole night. I was getting fairly decent attention from other girls, but nothing major.

I had a few dances here and there but I was getting nowhere really. At this time of my life, to go out and not get laid or find a potential date was absurd. That was the level of expectation I had for myself.

I also blame it a bit on peer pressure. All we talked about as guys while we were out was girls, or which girls we would smash or not smash and the girls we had smashed. For me with my reputation, my friends would look at me and be like "Rex hasn't got anything so we are okay". I became the benchmark for getting laid.

I had to grow and learn to live with that pressure. When the clock struck 3am and the lights came on in the club, that girl was around me again. This time she seemed like she wasn't going to give up. Well, the night was over and I had nothing better to go for.

I then accepted her offer of a kiss even though reluctantly. I was starting to feel better than what I felt -I should not be settling for less. I asked my friend Kenny if he would mind smashing her. He said he wouldn't mind. I was like "Okay, I guess I should". So I left the club with her. Her name was Erika and she was a tall Polish blonde. She was 32 and I was still 28 at the time.

I found out on our bus trip back to mine that she was a mother of two kids already. Okay then, maybe she could teach me a thing or two that I didn't know. Maybe there was something positive to come out of this I thought to myself. I was trying to find any positive in this situation as I didn't fancy her at all.

We got back to my place and I wasn't bothered about playing games or anything. I just said "Ok let's fuck as I am really tired". I didn't even take her into my bedroom, we stayed in the living room.

I normally had sex with the lights on, but for some reason I turned the lights off that day. We had sex for about 10 minutes in the dark and we were done. I turned the lights back on and everywhere was wet. She had squirted everywhere, all over the sofa, the couch and the walls.

I burst out laughing and I asked her "Was it really that good?" She was like "Yes, I hadn't had sex in six months". I was well and truly flattered. We cleaned up the squirt with towels and even a hair-dryer. What an experience. I felt sorry for Erika and the next day I took her for a nice breakfast and dropped her off at her home in North London.

ROW 38

ANOTHER NURSE

APRIL 2014

Erika texted me obsessively over the following weeks. For me though that was that. I was not attracted to her at all and I should never have slept with her. I imagined she needed a male companion as she had spent the last four years bringing up her two kids alone. I said "Erika I am sorry, that man is not me".

That last experience actually got me into researching squirting from women and I became a pro, so ever since I had a squirter after that I was never surprised. However, I had never had one on such insane waterfall scale enough to flood my whole living room.

I was invited to a gangster-themed party at a terrace bar called Upper West on Kings Road in Chelsea by an Italian socialite called Antonio. The party was full of girls and he wanted a bunch of guys to keep the girls entertained. This was my territory.

I am not a pro at fancy dress as you found out from my Halloween experience with Louise in the "My first true love" row. But on this occasion, I made a good effort. I put on a white shirt with a grey waistcoat and grey trousers along with a bowler-type hat. I looked pretty sharp and gangster.

I was at the party with a Russian friend of mine who I was just catching up with. His name was Ivan. For some reason he was not in the best form on the night and it seemed as though he scared every girl away.

I was getting along with this Swedish girl called Amanda, and Ivan was talking to her friend. He just didn't get it. His approach was so wrong. He even said something so offensive that the girl started crying.

There was nothing I could do to salvage the situation to be honest. I tried my best. The whole night was a fail. At the end of the night, I walked out pissed off with him. It just shows the importance of a great wingman.

When I got outside, I saw a girl leaving the club on her own. I spoke to her and asked how her night was. She said she was walking over to her cousin's place down the road and that I seem like a nice guy so I should come with her. Boom! Something out of nothing again. So I walked with her five minutes down the road.

Her name was Carla and she was half Spanish and a nurse. Yes, another nurse. I stayed at her cousin's for a drink and played with their cats. She must have loved me. I then left after we exchanged numbers.

Carla and I were texting for a few weeks and I asked her out on a date. We went for my favourite again. A burrito and a cocktail. We kissed so much in the restaurant that we were both so turned on. I didn't take her back as I had plans for later that evening. Again another plus point for me.

On the second date we met up for a Thai dinner. As I was getting older I was now becoming more mature and more civilised with dates. This was a very romantic one. After the Thai dinner, she asked me to come back to hers to drink some more and play a cool board game. I didn't think much of it I was like "Okay cool let's go".

We got back to her place after picking up a bottle of wine on the way. She laid out the board game on the table. It turned out it was a game called "Monogamy". I was absolutely shocked in a good way. Things were about to get even more exciting.

The game was for couples and was a way to tease each other in several suggestive and sexual ways with the challenge of finishing the game without having sex. We never finished.

I saw Carla several times after that and we kept seeing each other for a few months. I lost interest as I felt like she never made a contribution to anything we did together.

She never once bought me one drink even though we went on several dates and for several dinners. I had to do something about it as I felt that she was really taking advantage of me.

One evening, we went for dinner and a drink. She was rude to me when I tried to raise the issue with her. So like any sensible person who was being taken advantage of, after we had dinner and drinks in this restaurant, I said I was going to the bathroom but I left and never came back. I never saw her since.

ROW 39

THE PATIENT SPANIARD

APRIL 2014

I was now at a stage where I had a bit of a Spanish obsession. Carla was half Spanish, and she had the sexiest mole in the world. A female version of Enrique Iglesias if you like. I started to notice that on every Spanish or Italian looking girl I saw out and was specifically going for them on nights out. Let's say I now had a type, at least for a little while.

Back at the Roof Gardens in Kensington one Friday in April 2014, I was out with my colleagues Jez and Karl. We were in the outdoor area having our end of the week work piss-up.

There was a large Spanish group in front of us. There were around six girls and three guys. I dragged my friends to join the group and we politely introduced ourselves. They were very nice and welcoming to us. It turned out that they were out for one of the guys' birthdays.

I am not even a funny guy, but I became the joker in the group. I found myself saying one funny thing and so I had to live up to that impression by trying to make more jokes. I didn't do too badly thanks to the shots of tequila we had in-between.

I particularly got close to one of the girls. Her name was Angela. She was from Bilbao in the Basque region of Northern Spain. I spent the whole night with her. She was very real. I felt like the Spanish girls did not require any games at all. It's like she had made up her mind from the very onset if she liked me or not and then she worked from there.

There was no need for any games like ignoring each other, controlling eye contact and keeping distances. There was absolutely no need for any of that in this situation. I think I found this extremely refreshing. After putting in a lot of hard work and using my intelligence and being strategic with so many girls, it's nice for a girl to like and appreciate you straight away based on who you come across as.

I ended up going back to a Spanish shared house in Canary Wharf. This was the beginning of a year-long experience with Angela. She was really cool, very warm and very beautiful. She was also very patient with me. We became very good friends. I could call her if I needed anything or any help.

We saw each other every single week as I worked close to her house. I went over for lunch and sex at her place several times. She always felt like I was a player and knew I was seeing other girls. I think again she liked this about me and probably found it attractive. But at the same time, had I wanted to be exclusive and settle down, she would have been up for that too.

She was a very beautiful girl. One of the most naturally beautiful ones I have ever been with. The only reasons I felt we didn't end up together was that I felt she was a bit too relaxed about life and might have lacked ambitions to succeed in the same way I had.

ROW 40

BUNGA BUNGA

APRIL 2014

Whilst still seeing a few girls from the past I needed to have a little cull, so at this point, I think I ended it with and a couple of other girls. But while doing that there were more girls coming into the picture. It was becoming uncontrollable.

Sometimes I made up reasons to end things with girls. I said I was seeing someone else most of the time. This was fairly true. I never liked to be seeing more than four girls at once. I felt like anymore was definitely too much to deal with.

What I also noticed was that I found that I always had an order of preference. No matter how many girls I had on the go, there was always some sort of hierarchy. So I always managed things based on this order.
What determined my preference was things like appearance, how good the sex was and how much fun I had with them. All the obvious things.

To break it down a bit more or give you an example. Sometimes I would crave boobs, and I would want to meet up with the girl with the biggest or best boobs, sometimes a good ass, sometimes I would feel like a blowjob, and I would meet up with the one who gave the best blow job.

Based on that, I think I had not found a girl who ticked all my boxes. I think this was why I was able to continue seeing multiple girls at several points since my break up with Louise. I never found one person who satisfied every aspect for me.

I had a University reunion with my old housemate Alex as well as his Italian ex-girlfriend Daniella and her friend Francesca. We met up for a bottomless brunch at an Italian restaurant in Battersea called "Bunga Bunga". The restaurant was named after the famous wild parties of the ex-Italian Prime Minister Silvio Berlusconi.

We had a fun day, ate lots of pizza and sang karaoke, whilst drinking bottomless prosecco. We were basically set up like two couples. Alex and I took part in the karaoke and sang "Don't Cha" by The Pussycat Dolls featuring Busta Rhymes. We changed the word "Girlfriend" to "Boyfriend".

It was a very fun day. Even though we were set up like two couples, I still flirted with other girls and exchanged numbers. I was never going to assume Francesca was mine as I didn't know her. I stuck to the principles that had worked well for me so far.

Saying that, I did flirt with her a little bit. We were getting exponentially more drunk by the hour so that made it easier. I didn't kiss her until we got back to Alex's place in the evening.

By this time we were both pretty smashed. There was an awkward moment in the living room when Alex took Daniella into his room and we could hear them having sex. I joked with Francesca saying "do you want to go for a walk"? She was like "No, I want some of that too".

She jumped on me and rode me and we had sex while I was watching "Family Guy". Alex and I and the two Italian girls, we definitely had our own "Bunga Bunga" on that day.

ROW 41

FUTURE SMASH

APRIL 2014

Francesca went back to Italy as she was only in London for a long weekend. I didn't really bother keeping in touch with her as I felt there was no point in this case. Keeping in touch was definitely something I was extremely good at.

If I take you back a year to the "Stuck in Madrid" row from May 2013. I had actually gone out with Angelo and Richard on our second night and we went to Teatro Kapital, a nightclub in Madrid with seven floors.

We were on the third floor when I was approached by an English girl, Nicola, who was out there on a Hen-do. She was very keen to know who I was and to talk to me and dance with me. I get suspicious of single girls on hen-dos as I feel like they might feel a certain pressure and are looking for a guy to get married to in case they catch the Bouquet at the wedding.

For single guys on stag-dos, it's always more about messing about. Being playful, enjoying strip clubs, shagging girls, and having an all in all messy experience. I spoke to Nicola for a bit at the club, and we exchanged numbers with the intention of perhaps meeting up back home in England in the future.

The future here came a year later. I was bored one afternoon and I was going through my Whatsapp contacts and I decided to message her. She was so excited and surprised that I messaged her after so long. The truth was that I genuinely forgot.

I am sure she remembered me when she arrived back in London the previous year, but she probably expected and wanted me to message her first. I totally disagree with this logic as we are well into the 21st century and it shouldn't matter who sends the first message. Is it really worth missing out on somebody for silly games and rules like that?

It turned out we worked around the corner from each other at the time. We had about two or three lunch dates. We then had a fourth date for cocktails. It was a very happy hour. We went back to her place and we slept together for the first time, exactly after one year of meeting.

All this was triggered by me being proactive and digging into my contacts whilst searching for any untapped female potential on my phone.

I would recommend the guys and girls did this more often, as you never know what might have changed in people's lives over time. That guy or girl you didn't like two years ago might not be who you thought he/she was, or he/she might have had a life-changing experience to make him/her more the person you desire. You just never know. So we should never fully shut the doors on the people we meet if they haven't done anything bad to us.

ROW 42

DREAM COME TRUE

July 2014

I stayed in touch with Nicola for a while after that. She was probably very low in my pecking order of women. I never really saw anything happening with us, but I did like her boobs. So every time I had a boob craving, I would drop her a text, and she was more than happy to meet up. It was like Boobs on Demand.

It was July 2014 now time for more serious stuff. My friend Kyle was getting married, and so we had a stag-do trip planned in Marbella in the south of Spain. We made this an extended stag-do, with the main part of it taking place over one weekend. Eighteen of us flew out there and ten of us stayed there for a whole week.

We stayed in Puerto Banus, a nice lively area of the town near the harbour. We had booked out two private Villas next to each other. The stag-do was very messy. It involved typical laddish things. For example, Kyle, the stag had to pull a cork out of Joe's ass with his mouth. That's the sort of stuff that went on. He was also put through some Dominatrix style treatment involving whips and chains at a strip club in town.

After the strip club night, a few of us headed over to a bar called "Linekers". Things got even messier there. Cheap shots and cheap drinks meant more shots and more drinks naturally. I was feeling very good. Few of us made it out past midnight. I remember there been about four of us left. Myself, Kenny, Neil, and Paddy. We went to a club called "Kube". This was open a bit later than the others until about 6am.

On the dance floor at Kube, I saw a hot blonde with a stunning body. She was almost bimbo-like. She looked like a playboy bunny, almost. You don't often get to see girls who look like this out and about. This was definitely not an everyday occurrence for me and I had to make the most out of it.

I walked up to her confidently, I asked for her name. She said "Jessica". I smiled and literally had a very basic introductory conversation with her. I explained why I was there, I told her about my day. For her, I needed to come across as honest and genuine as she would have got more than enough attention all day every day. This worked like magic.

We started dancing. I was wearing jeans and no underwear and she could feel my erection. She asked "Do you always dance like this?" I replied "only with the right person". We both laughed about it and carried on dancing.

Jessica was gorgeous and so hot. I kept pinching myself. I kissed her in the club and we swapped numbers. I think I actually went further and asked her to come back with me that night. I was on holiday and only in Marbella for a few days, there was no time to play the long games. She was actually out with her mum so, I think that was the only reason she didn't come with me that night.

Jessica and I were texting right away from the next day. We arranged for her to come to the villa to hang out. She lived in Malaga and so she made the half an hour drive down to Puerto Banus. There was a bar next to the villa and we went there for a drink. I knew she was into me and I was definitely into her. I couldn't believe I was getting a chance with a girl who looked like that.

Going to the bar for a drink helped us build some chemistry and some desire for each other. I was taking it one step at a time to be honest. It actually almost felt too good to be true that I had a girl so stunning in front of me.

We had a couple of drinks, and I felt like it was a good time to take her to the villa. We walked down, and got in there. My friends all went out for a long lunch to keep the place free for me in case I got lucky. I played some music on the sound system in the living room and set the tone. I was assuming we were going to have sex, but I was just being presumptuous.

I started kissing her again and we started touching each other. She paused and said "I am not having sex with you". I froze in shock but then I quickly composed myself. She then followed up saying she would give me a blow job instead. At this point, I would have grabbed that option with both hands. Instead, she grabbed my penis with both hands and then performed oral sex on me.

That was as far as I got with Jessica on that day. I kept at it, I was making progress. Again we agreed to meet up in a couple of days. This time there was an element of romance. At this point, we were a smaller group of guys left in Marbella and so we moved to a hotel. The H10 Andalucia Plaza. Jessica picked me up from here and we drove to the beach and had some cocktails.

I was fairly relaxed and she kissed me and said "Let's go back to your hotel and have sex". Boom! I thought she was joking. I had done it. We headed back to the car park and she drove us back to the hotel where we had sex. We had sex about four more times on my stay there.

ROW 43

GOOGLE TRANSLATE

JULY 2014

Marbella was a very successful trip for me. Obviously, I met Jessica on one of the early nights of the trip, in the time I was waiting to sleep with her, I did sleep with a few other girls. I was definitely starting to hit my peak.

One evening when my friend Kenny and I were leaving our hotel to join the other guys out for a drink, we bumped into two girls in the lobby. They were Spanish and pretty much spoke no English. We managed to convince them to come for a drink with us using hand signs and making random sounds.

This would have been a very funny sight to any onlooker. Actually, I think the girl Kenny was speaking to spoke a bit of English. I was stuck with the one who spoke none at all. I must say this was very challenging. Basically, there was no way to communicate at this point. She was so hot though and I did not want to give up due to something so silly as not being able to communicate.

My plan was to get to the bar, buy the girls some drinks and make them feel comfortable. After all drinks and music are universal. If we could drink together and dance together that was good enough.

What I had forgotten was that on the iPhone in my pocket, I had a translate app. I was going to do whatever it took to make sure I gave it my best shot to try and get laid with this girl tonight. We went to a Latin nightclub on the harbour which played South American music as we knew the girls would like it. When we got to the bar, we got some drinks and shots of tequila.

I pulled out my phone, and opened "Google Translate". I found out her name was Darla, and she was 23. She was half Spanish, half Ecuadorian. She was studying to be an accountant. She had one older brother. Her parents were divorced and she didn't like her mum's new boyfriend. Her favourite song was "Bailando" by Enrique Iglesias featuring Gente De Zona, Sean Paul, and Descemer Bueno.
I am sure you can imagine how long every conversation we had would have taken as we both were basically writing on my phone in different languages and then translating it for the other person. It was actually so much fun and one of the most random experiences I have had. In terms of improvisation, it is definitely up there for me.

Darla probably had never had that sort of experience with a guy. As guys, we need to realise that attractive girls would also attract so many nice guys like us. This is inevitable. However, if you are able to stand out somehow and give a girl a different kind of experience, she will find you interesting. These are examples of things that we can do to stand out in the eye of the girl we want.

We stayed at the bar till about 2am. Very early for Spain. But at this point, we were getting on well with the girls. We had built up some good momentum and so we decided to head back to the hotel.

When we got back to the hotel, I dragged Darla straight back to my room and we went straight to the point. We literally got in, took our clothes off and had sex in the bathroom. There was no point doing anything else as our fingers were probably hurting from typing on Google Translate all night.

ROW 44

TWO HOTELS

JULY 2014

Yes, the next row on the spreadsheet still comes from Marbella. All through my twenties in my single years, on a standard weeklong holiday I would probably have sex with three girls on average. For example, I was really disappointed that I only had one in Ibiza. This was unacceptable. Marbella was going great though.

At this point, I was almost averaging one new shag a day. I felt like, "Wow, I should have come here earlier". Believe it or not, after the Madrid trip and this one, I started looking at Business Schools in Spain with a view to perhaps study for an MBA.

To take you back to the night before with Darla. After we slept together, I went back with her to meet her friend and Kenny in the lobby. Till today, I have no idea if they either got up to any mischief or not.

The next night, I was coming back from the club with two of the guys, Angelo of course and Nigel. We crossed the road from the main strip in Puerto Banus heading back to our hotel. We were on Julio Iglesias Avenue. The road had like a pavement in the middle with trees and benches. I spotted a brunette hottie on one of these benches. I had no hesitation in going over to talk to her. I approached her and she looked even prettier close up.

I sat next to her on the bench while my friends watched. Angelo sat on the opposite bench next to her friend. He might actually be the best wingman I have ever had as you notice by the number of times I have been successful with him around.

I introduced myself. Her name was Emily. The most beautiful Emily I had ever met in my life. Well, I obviously didn't tell her that but I was definitely thinking it. Obviously, I was a random stranger who approached her on the street at 4am. The priority as always is with me is to make her feel safe and comfortable.

Most guys when they meet a girl, they want to go all macho and stuff and try to impress the girl by trying to get their ego across. No that's not the way it should be. For me, once I make them feel safe and comfortable, everything after that just flows. At the end of the day, most women subconsciously want security from a man. Even from a man they have just met.

So, I sat and spoke to Emily, she was from Manchester, but lived in Malaga and worked in the marketing field. She was in Marbella for a conference and was staying in a hotel around the corner with her friend. We chatted on the bench for about half an hour. My friend Nigel had walked on as he was the fifth wheel at this point. Angelo wasn't making too much progress with her friend. He stayed around though and walked back with us to the girls' hotel.

We all sat on the hotel stairs for a bit. Emily definitely felt really comfortable with me at this point as she sat next to me but facing me with her legs across my lap. We were all cosy and kissing each other. I felt great. I felt like it was love at first sight. Obviously, I was intoxicated so that must have had a part to play.

Angelo walked back to our hotel. I walked into Emily's hotel with her and she said "Rex you can't come up as I am staying in a room with my colleague and we have to leave at 8am". At this point it was about 4:45 am. I said "That's fine I'll get another room". I walked to reception and paid for a room in her hotel.

She was worth it. So, you can imagine what happened next. She went up to her room and told me to wait in the lobby. So risky. She might never have come back and I had just paid for a room in her hotel when I already had my own hotel room with my friends. Ouch!

Ten minutes later, she came out of the elevator and walked towards me. She had changed into a nightdress and had a bag with toiletries. Boom! I was winning in life.

We went up to the new room and probably made out for half an hour. It was the longest and most pleasant foreplay of that holiday. And then we had sex until sunrise. She was petite and so easy to move around and try different positions with. The Kama Sutra was very much a reality in Spain that night.

We then fell asleep cuddling each other. This made my holiday and I thank Kyle for getting married and giving me the opportunity to have had such an incredible experience on his Stag-do.

ROW 45

THE LONDON FASHION WEEK MODEL

JULY 2014

Emily had left a black lace top in the hotel room, so I took that to my hotel. I messaged her about meeting up as I had three days left in Marbella. She then said she would drive down to see me and pick it up the next night. I was excited and looked forward to seeing her again.

The next day arrived and she cancelled on me and said she didn't know if she would be able to see me before I left. My reaction proved that no matter how experienced or good I thought I was with women, I was still human. I lost my composure and my temper and I started sending her horrible messages. I was really bitter as I had fallen for her. I was looking forward to seeing her again and potentially having what we had again. It clearly wasn't meant to be.

It was fine. I got over Emily quickly. Our next night out was to "Olivia Valere" in Marbella. Google it if you haven't already. It was an amazing venue with a very good crowd. The opportunity to drown any sorrows I had came quickly with all the vodka I drank that night. There was a point when all my friends had left and it was just me in the club. I think majority of them had left with girls.

I walked towards the exit and saw a hot brunette in the corner. I went over and spoke to her. She offered me some cocaine. I said I was okay and that I was heading back to my hotel. I made a false promise to do some coke with her if she came back to my hotel with it. She jumped at the opportunity. We dashed out of the club immediately. I don't know if she wanted me or the coke. Either way, I made the most of the situation.

In the taxi she said to me "by the way I'm not a slut and we are not doing anything". I said "Valerie, why do you have such a dirty mind". That was her name as she had told me earlier. She was a model from the Czech Republic who lived in London and was very active on the catwalk scene for some major fashion designers.

The taxi pulled up outside the hotel and she gave me the most passionate kiss. This was so surprising for someone who had just said she didn't want to do anything. I grabbed her and we went into the hotel.

I was sharing a room with Angelo. I knocked on the door. He had a girl in there. So, I came back out and we went to the basement of the hotel. She started taking cocaine. That got her so horny and she took all her clothes off and I fucked her there and then.

Angelo's girl was cheating on her boyfriend and she got embarrassed when we walked in on them about to have sex. So she left the room and ran out to her car just as he was about to put it inside her. He ran after her to the car park whilst still wearing his condom. Poor guy. Hilarious though.

I took Valerie back to the room and we had sex in the bathroom. It was great. Model sex was definitely at the next level. She laughed at how shortly I lasted when we did it under the stairs. She was so demanding and she had incredible stamina. She basically fucked me but I liked it.

ROW 46

EMERGENCY ROOM

JULY 2014

I messaged Valerie when I got back to London asking to meet up but she never replied. Meanwhile, before I left Marbella though there was still one more highlight. Is your jaw dropping yet? I was still there and I was still meeting girls and was having the week of my life.

On the very last night. All the boys were tired. We had a crazy week of drinking for seven days and nights in a row. Well, that wasn't all we did. We also chilled in the pool and played pool volleyball. We went on walks on the beach as well and did all the normal daytime stuff. Well most of us did.

I spent some of the days with girls as the night time wasn't enough for me. For example, Jessica came to the hotel a couple of times for some day sessions.

So, it was the very last night. We tried to make this one an early one. We only went to a bar called "Seven" and left at around 2am. Well, my friend Kenny had got with a girl. The girl had three friends.

Kenny dragged Brad and I to be his wingmen in order to secure the girl for him and make sure her friends were happy. Notice the mismatch in boys and girls.

There was one girl who became the seventh wheel in the group. We walked over to get food on the street corner.

The group of girls seemed very keen. Brad had chosen one so I had a choice of the last two. I chose one called Hannah. We got in a big taxi and headed back to the girl's apartment. It was a room with three beds. Two of the beds were next to each other. With the third adjacent to both. It was a fairly big room.

Bearing in mind Kenny basically made this happen for all of us by getting with his girl, Charlotte. Brad and I were quick to get into the thick of the action. Brad just started fucking his girl under the covers on one of the beds. Within a few minutes, I was fucking Hannah too. We were now fucking these girls at the same time on different beds in the same room. Incredible. Where was Kenny?

So, remember the seventh wheel. She started feeling sick all of a sudden and rolling on the floor in apparent pain. Remember I promised to share a story about the worst cock blocker I ever experienced earlier in the book. This was her.

Kenny was obviously quite horny as he watched me and Brad have sex under covers with our girls. The seventh wheel wouldn't stop though. She now started screaming. She said she needed to go to the hospital.

You won't believe it, Charlotte called a taxi, and they went to A & E (Accident and Emergency) at a hospital in Marbella. Brad and I carried on having sex with our girls. I must say the man has good moves in bed.

A couple of hours later, we were all asleep. Kenny, Charlotte and the seventh wheel came back into the room from the hospital. At this point, Brad and his girl were asleep on the adjacent bed. I was sleeping with Hannah on one of the two double beds which were joined together.

I pretended to still be asleep. Kenny and Charlotte jumped into bed next to me. That must have been the moment they were waiting for all night. They had put her friend to sleep on the sofa bed in the room.

They then started to have sex right next to me. I could see everything, but I pretended to be asleep. Charlotte's fingers even poked me in the eye at some point. I still pretended to be asleep so as not to ruin their long-awaited moment.

The next morning we laughed at how much of a good time we had. We went back to our hotel straight to breakfast after a hard night's work. Even harder for Kenny after ending up in A & E all because he wanted some holiday sex.

ROW 47

ABACUS

AUGUST 2014

For me and for my friends, the weeks after Marbella were about coming back to reality. Back to the hustle and bustle of London. The only girl I kept in touch with from Marbella was Jessica. She actually flew to London to see me one weekend in the weeks following.

Working in Banking has its perks, but I have also had some long bad days. There was one particular day in August 2014 where I had been at work all day till about 11pm. I texted my friend Gary and asked him to meet me at Abacus Nightclub in London. Abacus has now since been renamed "Forge".

The venue was the perfect place to make me feel better. It was only around the corner from work and it always had good groups of girls who were up for meeting men like me.

Gary agreed to meet at the venue. Do you have a friend who you know you can always ask to come out with you? And they would always be up for it. Gary was that for me. We met up and went straight in.

When I go out with him, we tend to do more walking than normal. We always had this sign with our fingers which meant "let's walk around". That basically meant "let's do laps around the club and find some nice girls. We did this once or twice and found one group of about six girls.

The girls were very into their dancing, so it was kind of easy entry. I just grabbed one of them by the arm to dance as she had some good moves. I was kind of torn between two sisters, Sarah and Laura. They were beautiful blondes and they were visiting London from Newcastle in the North of England.

There was one part of the night where I was dancing with both at the same time with me in-between. If only fantasies ever became a reality. Well, they do sometimes as you will find out at the end of the book. With the sisters I obviously had to choose one right there and then in the club. They looked pretty much alike, and I believe they were actually twins.

Again, I obviously had to choose one. The sooner I did, the better. I went for Sarah as she knew most of the songs I liked and she could dance. It was like we were best friends for an hour. She was even giving me a massage on the dancefloor after I told her about the day I had.

What an amazing way to wind down. It was nice enjoying the Northern Hospitality here in London. I was wishing I could have had that more often. I kissed Sarah. Her friends took probably a hundred pictures of us. It felt like we were famous and there were paparazzi around or something.

At the end of the night, we swapped numbers and she didn't want to come back with me as it was their last night in London and she didn't want to be without her friends. Remember the phrase I invented? "Future smash". I was about to turn Sarah into one.

We were texting for a few weeks. We then agreed to meet up two weeks later. I got the three-hour train up to Newcastle. It was a nice train ride with very good views.

When I arrived in Newcastle, we went for a drink with one of her friends who was also in London with her. I think this was just to make sure I wasn't some sort of scary psycho.

Once she felt comfortable with me, we went to a nice mini Golf Resort on the outskirts of Newcastle which she recommended and had booked for us to stay the night.

I have been in several situations where I think "What have I done to deserve this perfect moment". This was one of those. It was a very romantic weekend full of sex and great scenery. That long day at work definitely paid off as I wouldn't have been at Abacus on the night I met Sarah otherwise.

ROW 48

WATERLOO STATION

SEPTEMBER 2014

Sarah and I lived 300 miles apart. It was tough to keep things going. At that time it wasn't the type of thing I was ready to get involved in as I was loving my lifestyle too much. Work was also becoming very busy, so I was drinking a lot more. I was working hard and playing harder. At this point, I was maybe going out clubbing four times a week while working five days a week.

I was going to some of the best nightclubs in London. I was meeting the most beautiful girls everywhere. Nowhere was impossible for me to meet a girl. I had reached this status where any girl I spoke to showed interest. Even for girls who showed no interest in me at the start, at the end of the conversation, their tone would have changed. I was evolving.

One night after drinking in Canary Wharf. I was out with Nigel and a couple of other colleagues. We decided to go out into Central London from Canary Wharf where we were drinking after work. We got on the Jubilee line and got off at Waterloo Station to change to the Northern Line to go to Dstrkt Nightclub at Leicester Square.

We were on the travellator at Waterloo station, and I saw a girl come up behind us moving in the same direction. She was with her friends also. This had become an instinct. I literally made the move straight after spotting her.

I walked over and used the "Fast questions" tactic. "Where are you guys going tonight?" They replied. Then I said where we were going. The one I liked replied saying she always wanted to go there. That was a good answer showing she was keen.

I asked more questions. It was simple stuff but I was extremely confident when I asked them. "Where are you from?" "What are you doing in London?" The next question was for her number.

Absolutely no chat up lines with Charlotte. I don't believe in them at all. I actually walk up to girls not knowing what I'm going to say. I have actually walked up to a girl and said nothing and just laughed as she was too beautiful and I didn't know what to say. She found that cute and we even went on a date. So please throw all your chat up lines in the bin.

I met up with Charlotte the next day in Greenwich. I took her out for dinner and drinks. We then joined her student colleagues for a student night out in the pubs in the area. This was like a throwback for me as it had been a while since I had one of those.

After the night I went back with her to her Hall of Residence. We had great sex at night and in the morning. Honestly, I was wishing I had acquired these skills earlier in my life.

ROW 49

THE BEST I NEVER HAD

SEPTEMBER 2014

Charlotte was disappointed by my constant demand for sex when we were in bed in the morning. However, I couldn't help it. I had worked hard and got her. I have a very high sex drive and some mornings I could have sex four or five times in an hour. She found this an issue. Well, I am Rex Wood; you either love me or hate me.

In the area where I worked, there were a lot of pubs where I liked to drink. One of them was the "All Bar One" in Canary Wharf. This bar was always busy no matter what day of the week it was. After work, there were evenings when I would be on my way home. But I had to walk past the pub to get to the tube station. I would be tempted to stop off for a drink if I was with someone or if I saw someone I knew.

One of these evenings, I was walking past and I saw Angelo in there having a drink with his colleagues. I stopped to join them. Whilst drinking my beer I noticed a girl with amazing eyes a couple of tables down from us. We made eye contact and I smiled. She blushed so much. There you go. That's simple. Her blushing meant she fancied me. I didn't need a second invitation. I stopped looking at her for a while. Then I made eye contact again and then she smiled.

I waited and waited on this one. Maybe I waited too long, but I remained focused in control and didn't get carried away. It got to the point where she and her friends were about to leave the bar. She looked at me like "Are you going to come over at all?" Then I went over. I probably didn't even need to say anything and she would have given me her number.

I joked and said I only came to ask for the time as my watch had stopped working. I was in a silly and cocky mood I guess.

Again, I gave her the "Question-time" treatment and I took her number and saved it under "Anna All Bar One". She was from New Zealand. I always saved girls names with a label of what club, bar, city or country I met them in. I notice a lot of guys and girls do this nowadays too. This comes in very handy for future smashes or if you ever wanted to work your backlog.

Now, for the strangest part ever, we never went on a date. Two days later, she asked me to go over to her house. She shared a flat with another girl. The other girl had a guy around. So basically these girls had set up a double date at their home. They actually made a very nice dinner. Anna got drunk so quickly and she actually went up to her room quite early.

She texted me to come up two minutes later. She was laying in the bed naked. What the fuck! She was all set. Her body was stunning. She wanted me to fuck her. And that was exactly what I did and to the best of my ability as always.

ROW 50

BREAKING MAN-CODE

OCTOBER 2014

I fucked Anna on one more occasion, but then we had a silly argument in bed as she found out that I had fucked another girl right before I came to her house. I basically had sex with two girls back to back in about three hours. The other girl was Angela "The patient Spaniard".

Another month, another night out at the Irish pub O'Neills in Leicester Square. This night was pretty crap. We didn't get much attention from girls that night. It was pretty basic. We walked around the bar several times looking for girls. Nothing was happening. I think the frequent sex was starting to take its toll on me. I was having to manage a portfolio of girls and struggling to keep them all happy.

At the end of the night, we came out of the bar and I saw a very pretty blonde with a great body. I pointed her out to Gary and said he should go for it as I wasn't in the mood. He went for it and spoke to her. I saw her more close up and she was very nice. She was blonde and French. Her name was Nina.

Gary fucked her a few weeks after that and then they fell out. I am very ashamed of what I am about to say.

So Gary sent me a screenshot of a message from Nina saying she had the tendency to be obsessive. He sent the message in trust to me. But at this point, I think my penis brain was the more active brain in my body. He even said I shouldn't message her.

I didn't listen and I messaged Nina and arranged to meet up with her. There was a day I had to be at work in the early hours of the morning and so I got put up in a hotel in Canary Wharf near work.

Nina came and joined me here and we had sex there. She also came and stayed with me for two weeks at my place and I literally fucked her constantly for two weeks, night and day. Gary was disappointed in me for a while. I definitely understood. That's something I would never normally do.

Normally, when a guy has his eyes on a girl. If they are my friend I totally switch off from the girl and she becomes a no-go. I have to say though however, Nina's bum was great and I even admit to Gary nowadays that it was definitely worth it.

ROW 51

IT WAS ONLY A GAME

DECEMBER 2014

I did think about Nina a few times when I craved oral sex to be honest. We always went on a date every time I wanted one and it always turned out being great.

I eventually started to see some of the obsession Gary was talking about. She would turn up at my house at odd hours in the morning after a night out. She once turned up at my work because I didn't kiss her goodbye when I was leaving for work once. This was definitely very scary behaviour.

Back at work, I was out for drinks one evening with my colleagues. When we were in the taxi heading out to a club, my manager mentioned that we were getting a new girl joining the team. He showed us a picture of her on Facebook and most of the guys got excited.

The day the girl joined, she set all the pulses going in the team. My floor was very male heavy and there were very few females. So the demand for decent-looking women was very high.

From my point of view, I saw the way the guys reacted towards Lavinia. She was Italian from Naples in Southern Italy. She was average looking, I wouldn't say she was pretty. However, from my point of view, all the guys seemed to be interested in her. Again, I have testosterone and so my competitive spirit meant I wanted to be the guy who had her.

When we got introduced, I started off immediately making a flirty joke. I think I was asking how she could be Italian with such a bad tan or something like that. It got her laughing. She definitely remembered that. This was her first day which was a Monday.

On the Friday of that week, we had a team meeting with lots of pizza. There would have been the tendency to want to talk to an Italian girl when there is pizza around just to make a conversation. I saw a lot of the other guys talk about pizza to her. In this meeting, I didn't make eye contact once. I knew what I was doing. This was Rex at the top of his game.

Later that day she messaged me on the online chat at work asking a work-related question. I asked "who is this?" as I pretended I had forgotten who she was even though we were introduced four days earlier.
That Friday night, she had gone out for drinks with everyone. I got a phone call from my colleague Jez asking where I was and that Lavinia was looking for me. It was happening again.

That night on her first week at work, I kissed her by the River in Canary Wharf. By the Sunday of the same weekend, we had lunch and drinks together at a pub in North West London near where I lived.

We then went back to my place and had sex fourteen times in one day. Yes, this was a record for me. I did fuck her several times after that. We had sex in the office, in the shopping mall, in my car, in swimming pools, in trains, pretty much everywhere.

This was obviously only a game for me, but I was so ignorant of the potential effects of all this on her emotions. When I lost interest in her it was very difficult to break the bond we had created. The only way I could break the bond with her was to get with another girl in front of her and show her proof that I was sleeping with other girls. This was horrible.

I admit I didn't handle things in the best way possible and I was extremely insensitive in this situation. Ever since then I have stopped getting involved in relationships or flings just out of competition as it always ends messy or with guilt.

ROW 52

REX ST.PATRICK

DECEMBER 2014

It was the work Christmas party. I was still sleeping with Lavinia even though I wasn't too keen on her. There was another girl I had seen at work who I was interested in shagging. Her name was Suzanne. She was a Irish and a new joiner who was very bright. I trained her on something at work and I had all these weird fantasies and I can imagine she was having similar or worse.

I also saw Suzanne in the gym a couple of times, and she spoke and asked if I wanted to attend classes together sometime. She also asked me if I was with Lavinia. I said no we were just friends.

So on this evening, nothing could be hidden anymore. It was all about to be exposed. The Christmas party started off at the Four-Seasons Hotel in Canary Wharf. I started off spending the night with my colleagues including Lavinia. When I saw other guys give her attention I acted like I was with her just to put them off. This was very terrible. I had never, until this point, shown such a trait. But like I said it was just that spirit of competition that was leading me.

I liked being the guy who's fucking the girl that all the other guys would love to fuck. I actually remember several times I never thought much of a girl. But then if my friends thought she was hot, then I would want to go for her. It was perfectly nothing malicious. Looking at the way I was going, I had betrayed my friend Gary by sleeping with Nina behind his back, and now I was sleeping with a girl at work just because I wanted to be seen as the guy who was sleeping with her.

Anyway, on this night, Lavinia and I were getting along fairly well. I got more and more drunk. Suzanne also kept coming around a lot. I had organized the after-party at one of the many Tiki bars in London, Kanaloa in Chancery Lane.

At this bar everyone was loosening up a bit, Suzanne was getting closer. She came close to me and we spoke and I really don't remember who kissed the other person first. But then I was kissing her right next to Lavinia. This was extremely cruel. Suzanne just carried on kissing me. She didn't care. She probably also liked the fact that she was getting with me while knowing that other girls wanted to be with me. We humans are cruel sometimes are we not?

That night I saw Lavinia in the rain in tears while I got a taxi back to Suzanne's place and shagged her. I had to work in the same place as these two girls for another six months. I continued to shag both of them while I was there.

ROW 53

UNNECESSARY

JANUARY 2015

Seeing two girls at the same place of work ended up quite disastrous as they themselves became almost in it or the competition. It was a perfect remedy for disaster and one of the most regretful things I ever did. On the other hand, it also made me a very desirable man. It was my University bad character coming back to haunt me in my professional life. One thing I would always tell people to avoid at all costs.

I was back on my latin attraction phase. While out with Gary one night walking through Leicester Square as we did several times in our Twenties. He stopped off to talk to a group of girls. They turned out to be Italian. However, I had definitely seen more attractive girls in my life. Gary wouldn't listen.

But like the good wingman I am, I stayed around and helped him out while he spoke to the one he wanted. It's so strange as she was the least attractive girl in the group. This is what makes the world go round, isn't it? There is always someone who will find a certain person attractive. It's one of the beautiful sides of life I think.

We chatted to the girls outside the M&M store in Piccadilly Circus. A little bit of street game. Gary and I were the best at this after years of practicing since we met when we were 19.

He took his girl back to his, and obviously, I was wing-manning him by talking to her friend. I was getting bored as I did not find her attractive. Her name was Arianna. She was Italian from Milan.

I had been to Milan so we had some good conversations. I told her about a time when I was out at Holywood Nightclub in Corso Como and I was talking to a girl and I collapsed. I got carried outside by my friend Kenny and the bouncer. When I got outside I woke up and my first words were "Where is the girl?" Arianna loved the story. I walked with her to the bus stop and I took her number and we parted ways.

I took her number with pretty much no intention of using it. It was just a formality. However, when that other brain takes control, the number of someone I don't even fancy becomes valuable.

I usually played football every Wednesday and there was this one Wednesday when I was feeling a bit sexually frustrated. So after the game, I sat in my car at about 10pm. I sent my first text to Arianna asking if she wanted to meet up. She replied saying "Yes come around" and she sent me her address. To be honest, it didn't excite me that much. I just wanted to go and hang out and maybe potentially shag her. I knew she would want some as Gary had been shagging her friend.

I got to her place in Kensal Rise, it was a 2-bed flat which she shared with her friend. They were all giggly when I walked in. I knew they found it exciting. I had a drink with them and then she went straight to business and dragged me into her bedroom.

We started off kissing and then spooning and then we had sex. Guess what. She was another squirter. She had taken the sheets off the bed before we had sex. It's like she was expecting to squirt with me. Or maybe she just did that with everyone. I have had very few squirters but now two of them were girls I didn't want to even sleep with. I forced myself. Maybe that part turns them on even more in a subtle way

ROW 54

I SMASHED THE COFFEE GIRL

JANUARY 2015

The sex with Arianna had been okay. It was nice to know it was so good that she squirted, but I was starting to get fed up of having strangers' juices on me in bed. I hadn't even met the girl properly. A 10-minute wing man conversation. A five-minute walk to the bus stop. A 15-minute drink at her place, and then straight down to the action and then rain everywhere. It sounds fun but, I was having the first thoughts in my mind that I didn't like sleeping with random girls.

I had no restraint though. I was starting a new job in January 2015 when I was moving to another bank in London. I vowed I wouldn't sleep with anyone at work and I would keep work life separate to personal life. I had not even been there for two weeks when I noticed the girl who served my breakfast and coffee started giving me the eye.

She made it so obvious every single day, to the extent she knew what I would order and what time of the day I went for breakfast, for a coffee or for a snack. She was hot. Her name was Carlotta, yes another Italian. If you have ever come out with me you will notice I do speak a few words of Spanish (well a bit, I did learn some from the Google Translate experience with Darla), and

Italian. I learnt Italian from spending time with several Italian girls.

I would sometimes be getting a coffee and hear Carlotta talk about how attractive she thought I was. As I got older it seemed I worked less and less hard to get girls. I imagine I had perfected the aura and swagger and it all oozed off me. I could probably walk up to a girl and say nothing and she would take me to her bed. Well in my dreams maybe. Ha ha!. I hope you get the message though.

I flirted back with Carlotta every time she made my coffee or served me breakfast. She was a lovely girl and was also very caring. I didn't make any proper move to try and get with her until she went all out. One day I went to grab a coffee. Her colleague, the other Barista, Alberto handed me a napkin with some writing on it. I looked at it and it said "Carlotta 07XXXXXXXXX". Perfect. She had handed me herself on a napkin pretty much.

I didn't hesitate to message her a couple of days later and she agreed to go for a drink after work. I took her to O'Neill's in Leicester Square. Remember what I said about taking girls to places you are comfortable with? it works. You feel prolific, you know the environment, you know the feel. You know how far the bathroom is and how long it would take them to come back when they go, so you are not caught unawares. You are in control of everything. You are "The Man". Her man at that point in time.

We had a few drinks and watched the live band that was playing there that night. It was good fun. A very decent first date. She had to be up for work at 6am and so we didn't sleep together that night.

The following weekend I was going to Oslo with a few friends and Carlotta wanted to see me before I left for the weekend. She came round on Thursday night. She helped me pack and then we had pretty good sex in front of my full-length mirror. She was speaking in Italian during sex which made it even better. There is nothing better than hearing "Si, Si, Si, Siiiiiii" while pumping away. It was great fun and very pleasant.

ROW 55

TINDER GLOBE TROTTER

FEBRUARY 2015

After shagging Carlotta, she left my place at about 1am as I needed to finish packing as the Oslo trip was the following day after work. I didn't kick her out, she left voluntarily which was fine by me. The last thing I wanted was to start cuddling the coffee girl at work and then going to work and seeing her when I get my morning coffee with her being all emotional.

Work was over on Friday, I was all packed and set to fly to Oslo. I met up with my friends Matthew, Ray, Rufus, and Billy at Liverpool Street Station. From here we hopped on the train to Stansted Airport.

A few weeks before this the trip I had downloaded Tinder and I upgraded to the paid premium service. The service allowed me to be visible to girls in Oslo and swipe right or left from London.

I was loving this as I met some pretty interesting girls. One of them was Caroline, a hot Norwegian blonde. She took interest in me straight away and was even dominating the Tinder conversation. I told her I was on Tinder to get recommendations for clubs and bar in the city as I was coming there for the weekend.

The best part of this was I didn't even ask to meet up. Get it? She then asked where I was staying. I gave her details. She even asked me to buy her something from duty-free and she gave me the money when I was in Oslo. Believe it or not, when I arrived, she was waiting for me at my hotel. Amazing, right?

I was there with my friends so I wasn't just going to leave them to shag a girl when we were on a trip together and had just arrived. So I brought her out with us. I also wanted to build the chemistry, generate a bit of lust for each other. I found that Scandinavian girls are actually very straight forward. I loved this about her. She literally said to me "Rex, I can't wait to have sex with you when we get back to the hotel". Again I still tried not to get complacent and I stuck to my game.

We went out with the boys and I introduced her to all of them. We all had a great night out together. We got back to the hotel at about 3am on the first night and we slept together. The sex was decent. The next day, I was out with the boys again. I kind of didn't want to meet up with Caroline. But wisely, I kept the option open.

In the daytime, we went to the best brunch party I had ever been to in the whole world. It was the party brunch at Bølgen & Moi Briskeby. Absolutely incredible, the atmosphere, the crowd and the quality of the girls was amazing. Here I met a couple of girls I would have loved to stay in Oslo to follow up on.

I still kept the Caroline option open for night two to hedge my chances of sex that night. We headed to a club at night. We ended up just messing about. My friend Matthew was taking topless selfies with girls in the freezing arctic temperatures. I was still holding out that I would meet a girl and not see Caroline. She had been waiting all day to see me.

Eventually, at about 1am she threatened me saying she was going to bed and I should forget about seeing her. I told her to come and pick me up. She jumped in a taxi and picked me up within fifteen minutes. We went back to my hotel and had sex. She had to get up at about 7am on Sunday to head to work. But then she woke me up with oral sex and then she rode me one last time.

ROW 56

PERSUASION

MARCH 2015

There were certain things which I did which were causing a menace. One of them was going out with Gary to anywhere around Leicester Square. We were almost sure to get some girls.

We went to O'Neill's pub again. This time it was on a Thursday. We did the usual routine of walking around. We then chose to settle on the middle floor as it was the part of the bar with the most girls.

We were standing near the bar and I was about to order a double-whisky and diet coke. There was a group of girls next to us. They were American. One of them did the sexiest slut drop I have ever seen. With no hesitation, I tapped her and said "you are not a bad dancer". She loved it. That was it, she was now stuck with a chatty and "in the mood" Rex Wood for the whole bloody night.

Her name was Katelin and she was only in England for four months as part of her course at college. I caught her right in the middle of her time here. We had a great conversation and an even better dance. Conversations build good chemistry; this then makes the physical stuff even better. So always try to have a good conversation.

Gary, one of my trusted wingmen was speaking to her friend Kendra. She was also pretty with blue eyes, so he definitely did better here than the last time we met the Italians.

There was a lot of dancing going on. At one point, I felt like she was going to break my penis with her bum as she loved the bump n' grind style of dance. I kind of liked it too. The best part was when I just leaned back against a slot machine and she did all the dancing. It was nice and relaxing.

When O'Neill's shut, we asked the girls to come back with us I ordered an Uber from there to my place. In the Uber their mood changed. My girl was "the leader" of the two.

This part is extremely important. When you meet a bunch of girls in a group, it I highly essential that you identify the leader. She is the one the other girls listen to, the one they wouldn't make decisions without. The one whose opinion always counts. The one who leads the trips to the bathroom. The one who makes her friends take photos of her all night. That is the girl you need to please the most. Otherwise, you can read my book 300 times if you wish and make girls fall in love with you. But you won't go far if you don't learn to manage potential cock blocks.

In this situation, my girl Katelin was the cock-block. If it had been the other way round, we won't have been able to turn it around. So luckily it was my girl who it was. I had the skills to fix it and I definitely was going to use every single one of them.

We got out of the taxi at my place and the girls decided they were not coming in, for reasons I don't understand. I said okay that's fine, I went inside to change into grey tracksuit bottoms and got comfortable.

I came back out and they were waiting for a taxi. I asked them what they were worried about. My words were "if you think we want to have sex with you, you are making a big mistake". "We are not having sex. Period, so stop being babies and come and chill inside".

Thirty minutes later, I was fucking Katelin from behind while she had both hands pressed against my floor to ceiling wardrobe mirror. She was so loud, I heard Gary and Kendra giggling.

You could say I lied to get her to come in. But when she came in she was more than up for sex. She even enjoyed it more than me even though I fucking enjoyed it. Even more because of the way I turned things around.

Why girls are like this, we would never know. But if you focus on making them feel safe by addressing their fears and insecurities then you have a much better chance of smashing them as I proved with Katelin.

ROW 57

JACK THE RIPPER

MAY 2015

I never saw Katelin again. She went on a tour of Europe and I didn't really have time to chase her. It was all just physical attraction from the club and the way she danced. So I was happy leaving that one as a one-night stand.

It was May 2015 and it was the day of the UEFA Champions League final between Barcelona and Juventus. I went to watch the match in Clapham at my friend Jason's flat. It was a very good atmosphere with pizzas, chicken wings, beers and vodka flowing all evening.

After the game, we made the five-minute walk to one of the most iconic, guilty-pleasure nightclubs in London. Yes, Infernos. I had been there in the past, but not often enough. Hence it only appeared on the lower half of the spreadsheet. The night went really well. I remember going up to the stage and dancing in a little cube with a hot girl.

It was the last track of the night, I had a few dances here and there but nothing solid. The lights then came on and the music stopped. I was too good for a "last chance Lucy". Instead, I approached a pretty girl with an amazing ass. I approached her and said "Hi, how was your night?" with the best smile I could give. The lights were on now so it was really cute. Her name was Emily and she was a lawyer. Other than approaching her and say hi, I almost could not do that much to influence the situation.

She was basically cross-examining me while we walked from the dancefloor to the exit. She asked me for my name, who I was out with, how old I was, where I was from, where I lived, where I worked, why I was out. So many questions. I believed she then made her mind up based on that. It was almost as though she was a walking tinder. She probably swiped right on my face in the club, but I was perhaps too intoxicated to see it.

Emily was nice. Oh and that ass. One of my favourites ever. We went to her place and she said she didn't want to have sex. I agreed and said I wasn't that fussed about sex and I just wanted to get to know her a bit. In the morning we spooned. It was impossible for her not to be turned on with my hard-on on her ass and so we had amazing sex. So amazing that we broke her bed.

The best part about this was that she then went on to arrange our first date. It was a new one to me. I turned up and met her at Liverpool Street after work the following Friday. We had planned to split organizing the first date. She was to choose an activity and I was to choose a restaurant. I met up with her and the activity was the "Jack the Ripper" tour through Whitechapel. It was actually really cool as a history lesson, but very graphic and dark.

We then went for dinner at Iberica in Marylebone, one of my favourite Tapas places in London. After dinner, we went back to my place and she wanted me to fuck her from behind and so I did that all night and all morning.

Emily even took me with her on a work trip to Geneva Switzerland where we had an amazing romantic weekend which included couple spa treatments, nice dinners and hanging out by the lake. She was a keeper but I never kept her.

ROW 58

STRAIGHT TO THE POINT

JUNE 2015

I did regret not keeping Emily. I don't know what it was. She wanted to do too many couply things and she wanted to be exclusive. Again I was enjoying my life too much to agree to that and so I just stopped talking to her. We got on very well too. It was a shame.

I moved on with life, I got more active on Tinder. I had been on one or two dates here and there. I had a couple from other dating apps like Happn and Bumble as well. There was even a girl I matched on all three who was naked in my bed and nothing happened because she only wanted me to use my fingers and her to use her hands. I kicked her out of my place. I wasn't a 16-years-old in the cinema or theater where my only option was fingers and hands.

Another girl from Tinder told me she left her purse at work and ran up a silly bar tab before I arrived. Fair enough I was late for the date. I never paid the tab as I thought that was extremely disrespectful. The same girl also spent 24 hours in my bed after our first date and was naked and also didn't have sex with me.

She even made me miss my trip to Goodwood Festival of Speed as I stayed in bed with her hoping to get laid.

So I still definitely had some crap experiences from dating apps.

I had another Tinder date coming up. It was with a girl called Ellie. I went for drinks with my friends at "The Folly", a bar in London. I had a couple of drinks there before heading down to the date venue. It was a cocktail bar around the corner called B@1. They had a happy hour where you had two cocktails for the price of one. So that came in pretty handy.

Ellie arrived and we got a cocktail to start off the date. It was going pretty well. We sat by the windows with a good view of London Bridge and the Thames River. It was a romantic setting. We finished our first round of drinks, and I asked her what she wanted next. Her reply shocked me.

We had been at the bar for maybe half an hour and were just pretty much introducing ourselves. She said to me "Why don't we just get a bottle of wine and go back to yours?" I always had a response for whatever a girl had to say, but I wasn't prepared for this. She just wanted to have sex with me and she wanted it immediately, clearly.

I replied "No, I want to stay out for a bit". And that was what we did. We had about four drinks there and when we made our way across London to "The Roof Gardens" in Kensington, another of my comfort spots as you probably remember.

Honestly I was actually really turned off by that comment of hers, but eventually we did go to mine, she stayed the night and we had sex. When she left in the morning, I never contacted her again.

ROW 59

STOLEN

JUNE 2015

I was definitely getting more mature with the way I was dealing with women. My reaction to Ellie's request also proved this. When I was younger, if she asked to go back to mine at that point. I would have dropped my drink, and we would have jumped into a taxi and zoomed off home. I might even have just fucked her in the bathroom of the bar. This was the level of maturity I was getting to. It showed how much I had changed from the first row on the spreadsheet until now.

The old gang was back. Gary and I. We went for a burrito at Benito's Hat in Oxford Circus. From there we headed to our usual weeknight hunting ground. The touristy Leicester Square. We went to the "W" hotel for a quick drink and then we decided to go to the Grosvenor Casino. On our way there, we saw two girls standing outside "Bubba Gump Shrimp". I stopped and said "Let's go over".

We went over to the two girls. They seemed happy to see us. We asked what they were doing. They were actually waiting for a guy one of them met on Tinder. Hilarious. The guy was also bringing a friend for her friend. The girls' names were Siobhan and Nicky. They were from Dublin. I definitely had a lot of Irish history.

I said to them "we will wait with you until your date arrives". We spoke to then for ten minutes, and then her date arrived with his friend. I was ready to leave them to it, but then Siobhan turned around to her date and said "Actually we will stay with these guys". I was in shock. Her Tinder date kicked off and wanted to fight us. His friend held him back. Gary and I were loving this.

We innocently came to talk to the girls and were going to leave them once their dates arrived. Now all of a sudden they wanted to stay with us instead. We ushered the angry guy away. We then took the girls to Dstrkt nightclub. At the end of the night, we actually went our separate ways.

We met them on Sunday which was two days later. We went to a sports bar in Marylebone for lunch and to watch football. Afterwards, we all went back to mine. I shagged Siobhan in my room. The sex was even better than I was anticipating. It was so good that I went out with her the next night again and we had sex again afterwards. This time the neighbours got woken up as my whole bedroom was shaking at four in the morning.

The next day I nicely put her in an Uber to her hotel as I got the tube to work. What a gentleman Rex was becoming.

ROW 60

MISS DEMANDING

JULY 2015

I kept in touch with Siobhan actually. She came down with Nicky for my birthday party later on in the year. Again, I was always very good at keeping in touch with girls. Sometimes though, keeping in touch wasn't the best option. One example was with Carlotta from the row of 'I smashed the coffee girl'. After my Oslo weekend, I found out she had told people at work that we had slept together. I severed ties instantly and we never spoke again. She was distraught.

There were actually so many of the girls on the spreadsheet who I would not have dated. It's strange, I find it very difficult to find someone I would actually date. Perhaps it's because I meet all my girls in clubs. But even for girls I met on the street and at the tube station, I wouldn't date any. However, I definitely would shag them, as I did.

I struggle with girls who are very demanding. I can't stand it. I like easy-going girls who make me feel relaxed.

I went out with Angelo at Drury Nightclub. At the end of the night, we bumped into two girls outside. Sara and Nadine. I latched on to Sara and Angelo walked with

Nadine. We walked to the Hippodrome Casino in Leicester Square with them. My approach with Sara was basically just being nice and not after anything. I didn't even flirt. I saw she was a bit of a diva, but I did want to get in her pants.

We found out we actually lived five minutes' walk apart. This was excellent music to my ears. We shared an Uber back home that night. It dropped her off first and then took me home. I didn't try to get with her at all. I was investing in the future.

Again, not trying it on with Sara gave her trust and security from the first time. We met up one more time for dinner. Another time we went for drinks and I met a couple of her friends. The third time we were to meet up was in my bedroom.

She came over one evening after work before I went to play football. When she came over, she actually came into the bedroom and sat on the bed. I sat next to her and we went straight for it. She asked me to go down on her which I did. She was petite and I literally fucked her in the air. What a great session that was! We did have sex like that a few times afterwards.

There was nothing wrong with Sara, but I felt we would be better off as friends. I found her always complaining and demanding to go to certain types of places, or not liking certain kinds of people and certain things. Very demanding of 100% attention always and I struggled to deal with that.

ROW 61

THE BURNING MAN

SEPTEMBER 2015

I stayed in touch with Sara and we remained friends for a while. We did get on and we hung out a few times as friends. I even introduced her to one of my friends. They also slept together a few times. What a wingman I was.

Another summer came, it was time for another getaway. The destination this time was sunny Los Angeles with a drive up to Las Vegas following it. We were a large group again as always. There were fourteen of us.

We rented a massive Villa in West Hollywood. The villa had seventeen bedrooms, an indoor pool, and an outdoor pool. It also had an indoor basketball court and an outdoor basketball court. In the basement, there was a cinema and a nightclub. I spent most of my time either in the hot tub or on the USTA approved tennis court though. Women were not the only things I loved smashing. I also loved smashing tennis balls.

In LA, a few of us had got tickets to a pool party at the Standard hotel downtown. We went for a Mexican lunch and then we walked to the standard. The party was very different from what we had expected. We saw people with really cool tattoos and really cool outfits and stickers all over their bodies. It turned out it was a "Burning Man" decompression party. We had no idea what it was.

Burning man is an annual festival or gathering with takes place in the Nevada desert, it involves a temporary city being built and then completely removed. That's as far as I understood. It seemed very much about being artistic as well as actively promoting self-expression. It seemed really cool. So there we were, at a decompression pool party after the festival.

We met really cool people at this party. I kissed about four girls actually, most likely through my British accent. I didn't have to do any work or play any games. It was so much fun. At the end, I ended up with a girl called Dana. My friend Nigel actually got with her friend too. This was actually a coincidence. They had a third friend who actually attempted to be a major cock-block. But it didn't work, as the other girls had their own free will and self-expression. Hence Burning man, right? There you go.

We got in an Uber back with the girls. They came back to the house. We went straight to the hot tub. My girl, Dana, went straight to the kitchen and made some late night dinner. It was really cool. We all ate and then went back in the hot tub. It was Myself, Nigel and the two girls.

After a while, it was time for bed. I took Dana back to my room which had the most incredible view of LA as we were actually based right at the top Mount Olympus in West Hollywood.

Who wouldn't want to fuck me in a room with such a view? I fucked Dana overlooking the city of LA. It was beautiful. The best view of the sunrise moment I have ever lived through by far.

ROW 62

WIFEY FOR A NIGHT

SEPTEMBER 2015

I stayed in touch with Dana, she was lovely. I did see her again, but not in LA. You will find out where shortly.

So far, we had some good nights out. I remember having a really good time and loving the girls at Laurel Hardware on Santa Monica Boulevard on Saturday. Sunday was the burning man party where I met Dana. On Monday, we went to Sound Nightclub. Here, we also met so many cool people.

I was having a great time at Sound, and then at some point, I noticed a cute girl in the corner with her friend. She was sitting down, but she looked like she wanted to dance. I approached her and asked her to dance. She loved it. So this started with a dance. It was more a dance and a chat though.

I was able to multi-task dancing and talking. It was nice. Her name was Hannah and she was out with her friend who was in the city for a conference. Her friend was jet-lagged and so she wasn't having a great time. But the best part about her which I loved was that she didn't try to stop Hannah from having a good time. I really respected that.

We danced all night. My friends even left me out with her. I was having such a great time with this girl. In my drunk state, I was like "if I lived here, I would want you to be my girlfriend, you know".

The best part was now yet to come. Her lovely friend said she was tired and needed to get back. She came over to me and said "I trust you to take care of Hannah".

At this point, I knew I was taking her back home. Jackpot!!! I played it cool, we kept dancing and kissing on the dancefloor. It felt like we were the only ones in the club. It was actually quite romantic considering we had only just met.

Hannah was quite drunk at some point. She asked that we should go back. I said, "Let's wait for one more song". It felt good that I could do that to such an amazing looking girl.

We got in an Uber to the house. In the car, she fell asleep on my lap. When we got to the house, she asked me to give her a piggyback. I piggy-backed her all the way to the bed. She woke up when she saw how amazing the view from my room was.

We sat in my little balcony talking whilst drinking some water. We then hopped in bed and cuddled and then we made love. I say "made love" because if you witnessed it, you would have thought the same.

The next day, Hannah asked me how many of my friends were in the house. She then woke up and she went into the kitchen and made everyone breakfast. She also wrote a list of recommendations for restaurants and bars our last night in LA. She then left as she had to go to work that day.

ROW 63

ANTI-MONOGAMY

SEPTEMBER 2015

I won't lie, Hannah got me thinking. I was starting to become a different Rex. Things were changing. I still had my wild side of course. Trust me this wild side was still dominating. But it was nice to see that emotions I hadn't felt in a long time were still there.

We had an early morning drive to Sin City, Las Vegas the next day. So we didn't want our last night to be a big one. On Hannah's recommendation, we went for dinner at Cecconi's on Melrose Avenue. A very good Italian restaurant I must say.

It was time to hit up the tinder matches since I wasn't going to a club. At the top of my LA Tinder list was Jennifer, an anti-monogamist. We had spoken for weeks on Tinder from when I was in London. Yes, I did what I did before the Oslo trip again by getting Tinder premium. I was speaking to Jen about potentially meeting that night.

We made the two-minute walk from Cecconi's to Catch, a nice rooftop bar also on Melrose Avenue. Here we met a few more girls, but my energy levels were low. I had no drive or energy to chat up new girls.

Jen asked me to come over to her place. So I asked Nigel to come with me for safety. I had seen pictures and videos of her, but I wanted to avoid a catfish situation.

We arrived at her building. She asked me to come to the roof. But by getting a lift to the thirteenth floor and not the fourteenth which was the top floor. Nigel was worried. We eventually found our way to her rooftop via a ladder from the thirteenth floor. She was waiting patiently on the roof for me. Nigel stayed for a couple of minutes and then he left once it appeared that I was safe. See my friends are like brothers. We all look out for each other.

Jen and I spoke a bit with the aim of building chemistry before sex. Basically, our meet up was purposefully for sex as we had agreed that we would have sex if we liked each other. Jen was different from anyone I had ever met. She loved sex like I did. She didn't believe in monogamy. She believed anyone should have sex with anyone they wanted. This worked for me as she had one hell of a body, and it turned me on a lot hearing such refreshing views on life.

I am not saying I agree with any of it. I would definitely like to be married with kids and love someone for life. I would actually like to do that very soon.

We went into her apartment and she showed me round. It was actually in downtown LA and close to where I was for the burning man party. We got into her room and started kissing passionately. She then bent down and gave me oral sex. She gave me that for a long time actually. I can't remember receiving it for that long ever. She then asked to have sex in the shower. I lasted not long. It was quite embarrassing. She paused and said "it seems we are both tired, let's go to bed and have proper sex in the morning". She set an alarm for 6am.

When the alarm went, I was more than ready to go. Morning glory and all. It was the opposite of the night before. I had sex for Britain and I showed her that we British men give the best sex in the world. She was pretty sore afterwards but she enjoyed it. I did too.

ROW 64

MOLLY PERCOCETS

SEPTEMBER 2015

After sex, I left Jen's place a very happy man. I headed back to the house as I had to go and pack as we were making the four-hour drive to Las Vegas that morning.

We arrived in Vegas at about 3pm. It was my first time there. I was extremely excited. Some of the guys who had already arrived were already pretty drunk so we had some catching up to do. I went to my room, dropped my stuff and got on the drinks straight away. It was a great feeling being here. It was as if I was home.

We were staying at the Encore hotel, and our first night out there was at the Surrender nightclub. Before the night out, the single guys in our group went over to Sapphire strip club to whet our appetites for the night. I was actually very impressed by the quality of the staff there. I am not really a big fan of strip clubs normally. I was a fan of this one though.

I was wearing a white shirt and I didn't want the stripper's makeup to stain my shirt, so I bought a Sapphire night-club t-shirt and put that on for the dance I had. Speaking of stains, my friend Neil must have had the best dance of his life. The proof of this was the fact that he actually ejaculated in his boxers during a dance

with a stripper. What a legend! We were in the Sapphire for about an hour and then we went back in the limo to Surrender which was in the adjoining Wynn hotel.
We were out in Surrender and had a good table close to the dancefloor. There was a bachelorette party table next to us and the girls on there were nice and friendly, so we spent the time most of the night chatting to them. At the end of the night, a lot of the guys were extremely drunk.

Kenny slept on the chair in his room head on his lap, jeans halfway down his leg. Nigel was found in the hotel corridor passed out with his trouser off and all his belongings next to him. Wallet, phone, watch, shoes everything. Noah sleepwalked out of his room and was found by a security guard who alerted his brother Jim. Ray was trying to get a bottle of water from the vending machine and inserted his card into the Dollar bill slot. He lost his card.

I went to the bar with Jason to get some food and watch some football on TV. I was pretty smashed but not as bad as the other guys. I was able to have sex. Jason alerted me to a girl at the bar in a green dress. Her friend had gone off with a guy and she was waiting for her.

I went over and spoke to her. Her name was Louise. As I started talking to her, I realized she was gnashing her teeth together. It was hilarious. She was on pills. She asked if I want some. I had never taken pills in my life and I wasn't about to start.

I don't know what came over me. I had nothing to lose I guess. The words "I just want to fuck you" came out of my mouth. She went "Let's fucking do it". Her pupils were pretty dilated. She was fucked. She grabbed me by the hand and we went to my room.

I went to use the bathroom quickly before sex. She came in there with me and started trying to perform oral sex. However, she couldn't control her teeth, so I made her stop. We then just did it by the sink in the bathroom and then I offered her a glass of water and we both fell asleep. She woke up in the middle of the night and left. It seemed she had more of a sex drive than me that night with those drugs she had taken. I said to myself "Welcome to Vegas". This was truly becoming sin city.

ROW 65

CAESAR'S PALACE

SEPTEMBER 2015

I woke up the next day feeling proud of how hot Louise was. I couldn't stop thinking of how horny she was. I wish I could have had sober sex with her or at least sex where we were both the same level of "fucked". It wasn't to be as I didn't take any of her contact details. I could only hope I bumped into her again.

The next night out was at Drai's Beachclub and Nightclub. This time we had an even better table. It was behind the dancefloor with a middle bit where you could stand up and have a great view of the whole club. On the night we were there, the American singer "Lloyd" was performing. It was a fun night. I spoke to and danced with quite a few girls. I also made out with a few, most notably a hot Austrian nurse wearing a red dress. She was gorgeous, but I lost her.

Drai's had an after-party somewhere at the bottom floor of the building which we had to get an elevator to at about 4am. My memories at this point are very vague. I was in the elevator, and there were two girls behind me. They were cousins. One of them tapped me and said. My cousin likes you. Ha ha. Her cousin was right there, so it was hilarious. I don't remember much after that, but knowing my instincts while drunk, I would have hung out with them the whole time. I think the girls tried to gamble at that time, but they were both so smashed that they couldn't. They then asked me to go with them to their hotel.

I remember going with them to their hotel, the Caesar's Palace on the main strip in Vegas. It was the two cousins and another guy. It turned out that one cousin had got with a guy, and she wanted to find a guy for her friend to get with also. They saw me in the elevator and instantly decided I was the right guy. For all I know they might even have seen me in the club earlier. I imagine they probably would have. That was most likely when her mind was made up. There was nothing attractive about me in the elevator so I am pretty sure they had already made me a target.

We were two couples basically. We went to one of the restaurants in the hotel to get some food. I had Spaghetti Bolognese. This helped me to sober up a bit. We then went back to the girls' room. Both girls were Australian, mine was called Nadia. I think she was beautiful, I have no recollection of her face. I remember thinking she had nice legs also. We got back to their hotel and we just slept.

Morning glory again, I woke up. Her cousin and the other guy were obviously on the other bed so we had to be fairly quiet. We had the slowest sex I ever had. I had to tap her to come to the bathroom so I could fuck her properly. I did and then I dashed off back to my hotel.

ROW 66

CALI GREY GOOSE

SEPTEMBER 2015

I added Nadia on Facebook, I don't even know why. Vegas wasn't the place where you saw people again. It felt like everything was a one-night stand. But I could not help my retention instincts. I always wanted to retain every decent girl and have them for the future.

Our next night out was seeing Skrillex at XS Nightclub at the Encore hotel where we were staying. Some of us went to a different club, but I was with Neil, Kingsley, Kenny, Kyle, Paddy, and Jason. We had a table right next to the pool. It was a very good spot. There was also a barrier which meant no one could come to the pool without going through our table. So obviously we only approved for nice girls to come in.

At one point, I was standing up just taking a look around. I spotted a really cute, hot girl. I instantly reached over the barrier, grabbed her hand and then brought her into our area. She then started dancing like crazy. She was a great dancer. Definitely the best dancer on the spreadsheet.

My hands were all over her. She was wearing a short dress and my hands found their way to her pussy, out there in the open in front of everyone. We then made out like crazy. I sat down and she pretty much gave me a lap dance. At this point, I was so turned on. My friend Jason kept taking pictures and making videos.

Eventually, I couldn't take it anymore, I was extremely aroused. Lindsey was her name by the way and she was from California. I asked her "I am staying here at the Encore, Do you want to come back to my room?" She replied "No, thanks". Okay, I kept dancing and I waited ten minutes and I asked another question "Lindsey do you want to come up to my room to drink some vodka?". She replied "Yes...yes please".

We went up to my room. I had a bottle of Grey Goose in there. I poured her a glass. She had like two sips. I went close to her and started making out again. I slipped my fingers into her wet pussy. This was now the point of no return.

Earlier in the week, my friend Rufus had made a video of him having sex by the window overlooking the Vegas strip. I had the presence of mind to do it this time as I was not that drunk. I fucked Lindsey overlooking the strip from the 48th floor. It was pretty.

Lindsey stayed the night with me and we had morning sex. She then went to use the gym in the hotel and came back to my room after and we had afternoon sex. Afterwards, she came for lunch with my friends and I at the Bellagio for the buffet. She went back home to California later that day.

ROW 67

VANESSA CARLTON

SEPTEMBER 2015

"If I could fall into the sky, Do you think time would pass me by? Cos you know I'd walk a thousand miles if I could just see you tonight"

Great song by Vanessa Carlton right? Fuck a thousand miles, let's make it three thousand miles. Let me explain. It was Saturday in Vegas. We had a cabana at Encore Beachclub pool party. It was a great day. One of those which I look at pictures and it brings tears of joy. I was with my friends, the sun was shining. There was beer, champagne, and vodka flowing. The music was great, and most of all I was absolutely loving Vegas.

We had a group of 21-year-old girls who came to the party with us. There were about eighteen of them. They made our Cabana look the most enviable. We were just laughing around and playing drinking games. It was really cool.

Right at the end of the pool party, there were three girls who walked past our cabana and they were going to the next one. However, they saw us and came back. The girls had just cancelled their flights back to Florida where they were from. They were now going to stay two more nights in Vegas.

They told us that and we asked them to join us. I spoke to the one called Lisa and told her how beautiful her eyes were. It was Vegas you could say cheesy shit. Everyone was smashed.

Ray spoke to Sally, and Nigel spoke to Bridget. The other guys were nowhere to be found. I remember Matthew actually meeting a girl on the stairs at the exit. Later I heard he was shagging her within twenty minutes of meeting her. She had asked him if he would take care of her. I was proud of my squad. The guys were doing great. We were all a very confident bunch. The confidence of one or two spreads across the group which helps everyone.

We had these girls come out with us to Omnia Nightclub that night where Martin Garrix was playing. It was a great night. The highlight being Sally removing her bra to reveal her massive boobs through her fishnet. Matthew and Ray spent the night sucking on her boobs in the club. Right there and then. Incredible!

At the end of the night, I went back with Lisa. We had great sex. We woke up in the morning and had sex again and then we heard a female voice in Ray's room. Ray and I had adjoining rooms with a door in between. Lisa said that was definitely Sally's voice. We knocked on the door, and it was Sally in there. We had all fucked the three girls in the group we were talking to. I see why these girls cancelled their flight back.

So let's get to the Vanessa Carlton reference. After I came back from Vegas, I was still texting Lisa. She missed my penis so much that she booked a flight from Florida to come to London for 24 hours to hang out with me. I hosted her very well and she got her mileage worth in sex from me that weekend. Trust me.

ROW 68

REX 101

OCTOBER 2015

LA and Vegas were insane. Dana from LA drove up to see me on my last day in Vegas. I had the time of my life. I was now back in London and having withdrawal symptoms. I had the one weekend with Lisa which helped. My ego was also super-boosted that she did a "Vanessa Carlton" for me. She flew 3000 miles baby, for 24 hours with Rex Wood. That one trip actually elevated my confidence if I needed that. It showed me I could actually get with any girl no matter how hot she was. That year I was definitely doing very well for myself. I got with some very beautiful girls.

I looked through my phone to try and find some untapped potential. I flicked through some contacts I had not messaged. I bumped into one called "Emma Edinburgh Marbella". This was a girl I met in my hotel in Marbella. I met her in the lobby when I got back from a club where I chatted her up She was on her way to the airport to return to Edinburgh in Scotland where she was from. I still got her number as the world is a very small place.

I messaged her randomly saying "Long time, when are you coming to visit me in London?". She thought I was joking, but then I was able to talk to her for a week daily on WhatsApp. I convinced her to fly over to see me in London for a weekend. Are you observing the trend here? I was making girls fly from country to country just to see me. I was very flattered that she did that too.

Emma was young, she was about 21 and in her final year of University at the time. She really liked me. She even joked that when she needs a boyfriend after University she will come and find me and that our babies would be cute.

So I had her come to London and she stayed at my place. She was quite inexperienced and I actually had to teach her how to perform oral sex. She also only wanted to have sex in the Missionary position. Again I showed her different other positions. Sex with Emma felt more like a lesson than anything else.

I paid her a return visit to Edinburgh and she was actually much better in bed. We did keep in contact every now and then, but there wasn't more to it, to be honest. I would rather not spend my time in bed giving sex lessons.

THE END

MY BELLA

NOVEMBER 2016

Let me take you back for a moment. Let's go back to July 2013. In between when Rows 26 and 27, I went out to my usual spot, "The Roof Gardens" in Kensington. I was out with Gary, Dean, and Derrick. It was fairly good weather and we were outside.

I saw two girls walk past us. One of them was extremely beautiful with the most amazing long black hair. I went over to talk to them. Their names were Bella and Sarah.

It's funny, I was wearing my Gangster outfit which I ended up wearing to the fancy dress party in Row 38 "Another Nurse". It was a grey waistcoat and trousers with a fresh white shirt. I looked dapper.

So this girl had caught my eye, but it was proving difficult to get her attention. I tried all the basic things I knew. I tried general chit-chat. I tried my "Question time" tactic. Nothing worked, so I gave up.

I walked around the club with Gary and then we went outside again. It wasn't often I met a girl who tickled my fancy the way Bella did. Her friend Sarah had clicked on to the fact I was really interested in her friend. For some reason, my fear of constant rejection stopped me from going back to talk to her again.

Sarah pretended to faint while I could see them I rushed over. Yes, she did it so I could come over and it worked. Bella was there right in front of me. I looked her in the eye and asked "Do you like the venue?" She replied "Yes it's so pretty". I asked "Can I take you on a tour and show you round?". She agreed. I was ecstatic. At least she had opened up to me a bit. I had to work so hard to get her to let me show her around.

I showed her around. It was quite romantic as I held her hand and she was starting to feel safe with me. It was very nice. A great feeling. Something inside me made me feel like "I could be with this girl". I wanted to see her again.

She turned out to be from Newcastle and was only in London for the weekend. I asked politely for her number and gave her mine. I'll never forget that she saved her number on my phone as Beautiful Bella. A bit of a tautology as her name already meant "Beautiful". But you know what? You could fit in the word "Beautiful" in as many permutations or combinations as you like, but they would not be enough to describe her beauty in my eyes.

My best chance with Bella was just to try and keep texting her and maybe one day we would go on a date. Four months after meeting her, we went on our first date. I went up to Newcastle for the day and we had a nice day out. We went for lunch, to the market and for a walk along the Tyne River. Here we also had our first kiss. I worked so hard for this. I was delighted.

Three years later, I was still texting her every month. Every few months I would ask her if she wants to go to a show or a concert or go for dinner or anything that could possibly convince her to meet me. I also kept her involved with my life. I always briefed her on every girl I was seeing, and what was going well in my life and what wasn't. The truth was that I would have left any girl for her if I had the opportunity. I just have never felt the same thing about anyone like I do for Bella.

In October 2016, Thirty-Nine months after we met. I asked her the umpteenth time if she wanted to go on a second date. She agreed. I am very pleased to tell you that she is now my girlfriend. I am the happiest I have ever been. Persistence pays off.

See if you can match the rows below to the chapters

Date	Location	Approach	My Wingman	Place	Hair Colour	Nationality
Aug-05	Belfast	Me	Solo	Street	Brunette	Irish
Sep-05	London	Me	Gary	Uni	Red	Canadian
Mar-06	London	Me	Solo	Uni	Brunette	American
Apr-06	London	Her	N/A	uni	Ginger	English
May-06	London	Me	Solo	uni	Brunette	Welsh
Jun-06	Liverpool	Me	Dean	MSN	Brunette	English
Jul-06	Belfast	Her	Solo	Street	Brunette	Irish
Aug-06	Oxford	Her	Angelo	Work	Brunette	English
Sep-06	London	Her	N/A	JumpingJaks	Brunette	English
Sep-06	London	Her	Alex	Bus	Brunette	English
Oct-06	London	Me	John	Ministry Of Sour	Blonde	English
Jun-12	London	Me	Alex	Home	Blonde	English
Jul-12	London	Me	Gary	Kellys	Brunette	English
Jul-12	London	Me	Alex	Bliss	Brunette	Welsh
Aug-12	London	Me	Solo	Reflex	Blonde	Irish
Aug-12	London	Me	Harry	CharcoalGrill	Blonde	English
Aug-12	Mallorca	Me	Ed	Holiday	Brunette	English
Sep-12	Bournemouth	Her	Solo	Work	Blonde	English
Dec-12	Reading	Me	Dean	Union	Blonde	English
Feb-13	London	Me	Dean	Fez	Brunette	Australian
Mar-13	London	Me	Dean	Fez	Blonde	Irish
May-13	Madrid	Her	Angelo	Holiday	Brunette	American
May-13	Madrid	Me	Amanda	Holiday	Blonde	Spanish
May-13	London	Her	Richard	Jalouse	Brunette	Irish
Jun-13	London	Her	Richard	Home	Brunette	Armenian
Sep-13	Ibiza	Me	Angelo	Ibiza	Blonde	English
Nov-13	London	Her	Angelo	Verve	Blonde	American
Nov-13	London	Her	Angelo	Roof	Brunette	English
Nov-13	London	Her	Solo	Roof	Brunette	American
Dec-13	London	Me	Solo	Roof	Brunette	Spanish
Jan-14	London	Me	Kenny	Roof	Blonde	English
Feb-14	London	Me	Jez	Oneills	Blonde	Norwegian
Feb-14	London	Me	Jez	Oneills	Blonde	Canadian
Mar-14	London	Me	Angelo	Cafe	Brunette	American
Mar-14	London	Me	ingmanned a Strang	Street	Brunette	English
Mar-14	London	Me	Chris	Ballroom	Blonde	Polish
Apr-14	London	Me	Ivan	Upperwest	Brunette	Spanish
Apr-14	London	Me	Jez	Roof	Brunette	Spanish
Apr-14	London	Me	Alex	Home	Brunette	Italian
Apr-14	London	Me	Angelo	Holiday	Brunette	English
May-14	Marbella	Me	Kenny	Holiday	Brunette	Spanish
Jul-14	Marbella	Me	Solo	Holiday	Blonde	German
Jul-14	Marbella	Me	Angelo	Holiday	Brunette	English
Jul-14	Marbella	Me	Solo	Holiday	Brunette	Slovakian
Jul-14	Marbella	Me	Kenny	Holiday	Blonde	Welsh
Jul-14	Newcastle	Me	Gary	Abacus	Brunette	Scottish
Aug-14	London	Me	Nigel	Tube	Brunette	English
Sep-14	London	Me	Angelo	Wharf	Brunette	New Zealander
Sep-14	London	Me	Gary	Oneills	Blonde	French
Oct-14	London	Me	Solo	Work	Brunette	Italian
Dec-14	London	Me	Solo	Ip	Blonde	Irish
Dec-14	London	Me	Gary	Street	Brunette	Italian
Jan-15	London	Me	Solo	DB	Brunette	Italian
Jan-15	Oslo	Me	Tinder	Holiday	Blonde	Norwegian
Feb-15	London	Me	Gary	Infernos	Blonde	American
Mar-15	London	Me	Solo	Infernos	Brunette	English
May-15	London	Tinder	Tinder	Uni	Blonde	English
Jun-15	London	Me	Gary	Picc Circ	Blonde	Irish
Jun-15	London	Me	Angelo	Drury	Blonde	Spanish
Jul-15	LA	Me	Matthew	Holiday	Brunette	American
Aug-15	LA	Me	Ray	Holiday	Brunette	American
Aug-15	LA	Tinder	Tinder	Holiday	Red	American
Aug-15	Vegas	Me	Solo	Holiday	Brunette	American
Aug-15	Vegas	Me	Ray	Holiday	Brunette	American
Aug-15	Vegas	Me	Jason	Holiday	Brunette	American
Aug-15	Vegas	Me	Solo	Holiday	Brunette	Australian
Aug-15	London	Me	Nigel	Marb	Brunette	Scottish
Sep-15	London	Me	Gary	Roof	Brunette	English

Sexcellence Stats: The top fives

Top 5 Wingmen

Row Labels	Count of Name
Solo	16
Angelo	10
Gary	8
Dean	4
Alex	4

By Nationality

Row Labels	Count of Name
English	22
American	12
Irish	7
Spanish	6
Italian	4

By Location

Row Labels	Count of Name
London	44
Marbella	5
Vegas	4
LA	3
Belfast	2
Madrid	2

By Hair colour

Row Labels	Count of Name
Brunette	42
Blonde	23
Red	2
Ginger	1

ACKNOWLEDGEMENTS

I would like to thank all my friends, boys, and girls. Without you there would have been nothing to put into the spreadsheet.

My main wingman on most of the Rows, Angelo. You know who you are. You inspired me as an author. I appreciate it. To all my other wingmen. I can't name you all but you know who you are. I would like to thank everyone who made suggestions about what to do with my spreadsheet over the years.

Many thanks also to my illustrator, Jennifer Slater. Your creativity is incredible. Also countless thanks to my editor, Wendy Elvis for those long transatlantic late nights.

Finally, I would like to thank you my Bella for giving me permission to publish this book. Even though you didn't approve of the contents, you knew it was a dream of mine for a long time. I appreciate your love and support. Thank You and I love you.

Printed in Great Britain
by Amazon